CONTENTS

JEREMIAH
BIBLE STUDY SERIES

ACTS

THE BIRTH OF THE CHURCH

DR. DAVID JEREMIAH

Prepared by Peachtree Publishing Services

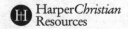
HarperChristian
Resources

Acts
Jeremiah Bible Study Series

Requests for information should be addressed to:
HarperChristian Resources, 3900 Sparks Dr. SE, Grand Rapids, Michigan 49546.

ISBN 978-0-310-09160-8 (softcover)
ISBN 978-0-310-09161-5 (ebook)

Produced with assistance of Peachtree Publishing Service (www.PeachtreePublishingServices.com). Project staff include Christopher D. Hudson, Randy Southern, and Peter Blankenship.

Thomas Nelson titles may be purchased in bulk for educational, business, fundraising, or sales promotional use. For information, please e-mail SpecialMarkets@ThomasNelson.com.

23 24 25 26 27 LBC 14 13 12 11 10

INTRODUCTION TO
The Acts of the Apostles

"You shall be witnesses to Me in Jerusalem, and in all Judea and Samaria, and to the end of the earth" (Acts 1:8). The vision was inspiring. The goal was lofty. How could the disciples act on these final words from Jesus and make them a reality? How could they undertake such an ambitious assignment to become the kind of witnesses that Jesus had called them to be? In the Acts of the Apostles, we discover the answer from those who literally wrote the book on the subject—and discover one of the greatest success stories in the Bible. We are inspired by their boldness and marvel at their adventures. Yet we also catch glimpses of their moments of weakness and doubt. We see major setbacks, poor decisions, and petty squabbles . . . and quickly come to realize these heroes of the faith—who spread the gospel of Jesus Christ and laid the groundwork for the church—were *very* much like us. We also come to realize the same Holy Spirit who guided them dwells within followers of Christ today. And we start to wonder what God might accomplish through our lives if we just gave Him the opportunity.

AUTHOR AND DATE

The writer of Acts does not identify himself by name. However, he refers to a "former account" and dedicates his book to a man named Theophilus (see 1:1). Scholars believe this former account refers to the Gospel of Luke—also dedicated to Theophilus (see Luke 1:3)—and given that the language, style, and structure of the two books are so similar, it is clear both books were penned by the same author. The early church fathers—including Irenaeus, Tertullian, Clement of Alexandria, and Origen—all concurred both Acts and the "former account" were written by Luke, a second-generation follower of Christ who was in a position to investigate the history of the early church and recount firsthand his travels with Paul. It is likely Luke wrote Acts when Paul was under house arrest in Rome awaiting his trial before Caesar, as Luke does not recount any further information after that point. This would place the date for writing sometime after AD 70, when the Gospel of Luke was composed, from the city of Rome.

BACKGROUND AND SETTING

The persecution of Christians was intensifying at the time Luke wrote both his Gospel and the Acts of the Apostles. Stephen and James had been executed, Peter and John had been arrested on many occasions, and Paul had faced imprisonment, false accusations, riots, beatings, and attempts on his life. Luke wrote his Gospel to record the acts of Jesus and provide an overview of what the apostles had seen and heard. Luke wrote Acts to provide a record of the acts of the apostles in the early church and to show how they sought to fulfill the Great Commission that had been given to them by Christ. Luke's recap of the first three decades of the church would have encouraged believers to consider and take comfort from the brief but rich history of Christianity. His message was unmistakable: God had blessed the efforts of His people to spread the gospel . . . and would continue to do so, no matter who tried to stop them.

KEY THEMES

Several key themes are prominent in the book of Acts. The first theme is that *the apostles focused on evangelism.* Luke witnessed the most fertile period of outreach in the history of Christianity. Churches were planted near and far, and believers were added to the ranks daily. The excitement, and danger, surrounding this evangelism explosion was palpable. Acts follows the early church through its infancy to its emergence as an agent of change in the world.

A second theme is that *the apostles had experienced personal transformation*. The men and women who spread the gospel and established the early church were thoroughly changed individuals. Nowhere is this more evident than in the lives of the two central figures in the book. In the Acts narrative, Peter, the disciple best known in the Gospels for denying Jesus three times, embraces the role of fearless leader that Jesus envisioned for him. And Paul, the staunchest enemy of Christianity, becomes its greatest defender.

A third theme is that *the apostles faced opposition with boldness*. The early church faced two enemies: the Jewish religious leaders and the Roman Empire. The book of Acts contains story after story of the attempts of these two groups to suppress, undermine, and kill off the Christian faith by any means. The courage of individuals such as Stephen, James, Peter, John, Paul, Silas, Barnabas, and others in the face of such attack galvanized the church. The body of Christ became a force to be reckoned with by its enemies.

A fourth theme is that *the apostles relied on the power of the Holy Spirit*. The arrival of the Holy Spirit, as recorded in Acts 2, provides the catalyst for everything that follows. Peter, John, Paul, and the other disciples were able to perform miracles as part of their ministry through the power of the Holy Spirit. Paul was guided in his missionary journeys by the Holy Spirit, who forbade him from entering certain places and warned him of the consequences of visiting others. The convicting, nurturing, empowering, and guiding work of the Holy Spirit in the lives of believers runs like a constant thread throughout the book of Acts.

KEY APPLICATIONS

Luke reveals how God places a premium on the *spread of the gospel* and blesses the efforts of those who seek to make disciples of all nations. He reveals how the *Holy Spirit* guides believers' words, gives them wisdom, and bolsters their courage. And he shows how God doesn't shield His followers from opposition but *accompanies them through it*—using trials and obstacles to sharpen their faith and make them more effective instruments for His work.

THE DAY OF PENTECOST

Acts 1:1–2:47

GETTING STARTED

How do you respond to times of waiting in your life? Why do you think God so often calls His followers to wait before He directs them to the next steps to take?

_____

_____

_____

_____

_____

_____

_____

_____

_____

_____

_____

SETTING THE STAGE

The Gospel of Matthew records that after Jesus' death and resurrection, He gathered His followers together and instructed them to "go and make disciples of all nations, baptizing them in the name of the Father and of the Son and of the Holy Spirit, and teaching them to obey everything I have commanded you" (28:19–20). In the Acts of the Apostles, we are a given a glimpse into how these followers of Christ began to act on these words and spread the gospel "in Jerusalem, and in all Judea and Samaria, and to the end of the earth" (1:8).

Jesus knew, however, that His followers would not be able to carry out this great commission in their own strength. So, before He ascended into heaven, He told them "not to depart from Jerusalem, but to wait for the Promise of the Father" (1:4). Once Jesus had left the earth, these followers dutifully gathered in an upper room in Jerusalem . . . and waited. Little happened until the Day of Pentecost, when the Holy Spirit suddenly descended on them, inflaming their hearts and transforming them into bold witnesses of the gospel.

The power of the Holy Spirit on that first Pentecost must have been both terrifying and exhilarating for those who experienced it. The sound of the rushing wind and the appearance of fire served as physical evidence of the Holy Spirit's presence and power among the believers. However, as we will see later in Acts (and in our own lives), the Holy Spirit often works quietly, subtly transforming the lives of believers without great fanfare.

It is clear from Jesus' own words that God longs to share His Spirit with people, if only they will ask: "If you then, being evil, know how to give good gifts to your children, how much more will your heavenly Father give the Holy Spirit to those who ask Him!" (Luke 11:13). It is also clear the Holy Spirit can transform the trajectory of our lives and enable us to glorify God.

EXPLORING THE TEXT

Jesus Ascends to Heaven (Acts 1:4–14)

---

⁴ And being assembled together with them, He commanded them not to depart from Jerusalem, but to wait for the Promise of the Father, "which," He said, "you have heard from Me; ⁵ for John truly baptized with water, but you shall be baptized with the Holy Spirit not many

days from now." ⁶ Therefore, when they had come together, they asked Him, saying, "Lord, will You at this time restore the kingdom to Israel?" ⁷ And He said to them, "It is not for you to know times or seasons which the Father has put in His own authority. ⁸ But you shall receive power when the Holy Spirit has come upon you; and you shall be witnesses to Me in Jerusalem, and in all Judea and Samaria, and to the end of the earth."

⁹ Now when He had spoken these things, while they watched, He was taken up, and a cloud received Him out of their sight. ¹⁰ And while they looked steadfastly toward heaven as He went up, behold, two men stood by them in white apparel, ¹¹ who also said, "Men of Galilee, why do you stand gazing up into heaven? This same Jesus, who was taken up from you into heaven, will so come in like manner as you saw Him go into heaven."

¹² Then they returned to Jerusalem from the mount called Olivet, which is near Jerusalem, a Sabbath day's journey. ¹³ And when they had entered, they went up into the upper room where they were staying: Peter, James, John, and Andrew; Philip and Thomas; Bartholomew and Matthew; James the son of Alphaeus and Simon the Zealot; and Judas the son of James. ¹⁴ These all continued with one accord in prayer and supplication, with the women and Mary the mother of Jesus, and with His brothers.

---

1. John the Baptist had said, "I indeed baptize you with water; but One mightier than I is coming. . . . He will baptize you with the Holy Spirit and fire" (Luke 3:16). What promise concerning this baptism of the Holy Spirit was Jesus now giving (see Acts 1:7–8)?

_____

_____

_____

_____

_____

2. What did Jesus' followers do after He ascended to heaven? What evidence does Luke provide that they obeyed His final command to them (see verses 12–14)?

_____

_____

_____

_____

_____

The Arrival of the Holy Spirit (Acts 2:1–13)

¹ When the Day of Pentecost had fully come, they were all with one accord in one place. ² And suddenly there came a sound from heaven, as of a rushing mighty wind, and it filled the whole house where they were sitting. ³ Then there appeared to them divided tongues, as of fire, and one sat upon each of them. ⁴ And they were all filled with the Holy Spirit and began to speak with other tongues, as the Spirit gave them utterance.

⁵ And there were dwelling in Jerusalem Jews, devout men, from every nation under heaven. ⁶ And when this sound occurred, the multitude came together, and were confused, because everyone heard them speak in his own language. ⁷ Then they were all amazed and marveled, saying to one another, "Look, are not all these who speak Galileans? ⁸ And how is it that we hear, each in our own language in which we were born? ⁹ Parthians and Medes and Elamites, those dwelling in Mesopotamia, Judea and Cappadocia, Pontus and Asia, ¹⁰ Phrygia and Pamphylia, Egypt and the parts of Libya adjoining Cyrene, visitors from Rome, both Jews and proselytes, ¹¹ Cretans and Arabs—we hear them speaking in our own tongues the wonderful works of God." ¹² So they were all amazed and perplexed, saying to one another, "Whatever could this mean?"

¹³ Others mocking said, "They are full of new wine."

3. What signs accompanied the arrival of the Holy Spirit in the upper room in Jerusalem (see verses 1–4)?

_____

_____

_____

_____

_____

4. How did the people in Jerusalem respond when they heard the followers of Jesus speaking in their language (see verses 7–13)?

_____

_____

_____

_____

_____

Peter's Sermon (Acts 2:14–24)

14 But Peter, standing up with the eleven, raised his voice and said to them, "Men of Judea and all who dwell in Jerusalem, let this be known to you, and heed my words. 15 For these are not drunk, as you suppose, since it is only the third hour of the day. 16 But this is what was spoken by the prophet Joel:

17 'And it shall come to pass in the last days, says God,
That I will pour out of My Spirit on all flesh;
Your sons and your daughters shall prophesy,
Your young men shall see visions,
Your old men shall dream dreams.

18 And on My menservants and on My maidservants
I will pour out My Spirit in those days;
And they shall prophesy.
19 I will show wonders in heaven above
And signs in the earth beneath:
Blood and fire and vapor of smoke.
20 The sun shall be turned into darkness,
And the moon into blood,
Before the coming of the great and awesome day of the Lord.
21 And it shall come to pass
That whoever calls on the name of the Lord
Shall be saved.'

22 "Men of Israel, hear these words: Jesus of Nazareth, a Man attested by God to you by miracles, wonders, and signs which God did through Him in your midst, as you yourselves also know—23 Him, being delivered by the determined purpose and foreknowledge of God, you have taken by lawless hands, have crucified, and put to death; 24 whom God raised up, having loosed the pains of death, because it was not possible that He should be held by it."

---

5. Peter had been so fearful when Jesus was arrested that he denied even knowing his Lord three times (see Luke 22:54–62). How would you describe Peter at this point? What do you believe caused this radical change in him?

_____

_____

_____

_____

_____

_____

6. How did Peter link Joel's prophecy with the death and resurrection of Christ? What promise is given for those who call on the name of Jesus for salvation (see Acts 2:21–24)?

_____

_____

_____

_____

_____

The Birth of the Church (Acts 2:36–47)

[36] "Therefore let all the house of Israel know assuredly that God has made this Jesus, whom you crucified, both Lord and Christ."

[37] Now when they heard this, they were cut to the heart, and said to Peter and the rest of the apostles, "Men and brethren, what shall we do?"

[38] Then Peter said to them, "Repent, and let every one of you be baptized in the name of Jesus Christ for the remission of sins; and you shall receive the gift of the Holy Spirit. [39] For the promise is to you and to your children, and to all who are afar off, as many as the Lord our God will call."

[40] And with many other words he testified and exhorted them, saying, "Be saved from this perverse generation." [41] Then those who gladly received his word were baptized; and that day about three thousand souls were added to them. [42] And they continued steadfastly in the apostles' doctrine and fellowship, in the breaking of bread, and in prayers. [43] Then fear came upon every soul, and many wonders and signs were done through the apostles. [44] Now all who believed were together, and had all things in common, [45] and sold their possessions and goods, and divided them among all, as anyone had need.

[46] So continuing daily with one accord in the temple, and breaking bread from house to house, they ate their food with gladness

and simplicity of heart, ⁴⁷ praising God and having favor with all the people. And the Lord added to the church daily those who were being saved.

---

7. Those who heard Peter's message were "cut to the heart" and asked how they could be saved. What instructions and promise did Peter give them (see verses 38–39)?

_____

_____

_____

_____

_____

8. How does Luke describe the birth of the church? What did this first fellowship of believers look like (see verses 41–47)?

_____

_____

_____

_____

_____

REVIEWING THE STORY

The followers of Jesus gathered together in an upper room in obedience to His final command and waited for the coming of the Holy Spirit. On the Day of Pentecost, the Holy Spirit descended on them with the sound of a rushing wind. Tongues of fire appeared above their heads, and they were suddenly able to speak in the languages of the foreigners who had also come to Jerusalem. Peter seized the opportunity to deliver a sermon, in which he connected the Old Testament prophecies of Joel and the writings of David to the risen Jesus. Some 3,000 people responded to Peter's message. The early church grew not just in numbers but also in fellowship. Believers pooled their resources and shared what they had with each other.

9. What was the angels' message to the believers after they had watched Jesus ascend into heaven (see Acts 1:9–11)?

_____

_____

_____

_____

_____

10. What did the believers do that both amazed and confused the multitudes (see Acts 2:5–7)?

_____

_____

_____

_____

_____

11. What did Peter say that the people had done to their Messiah (see Acts 2:22–24)?

_____

_____

_____

_____

_____

_____

12. How did God reward the efforts of His servants to spread the gospel (see Acts 2:47)?

_____

_____

_____

_____

_____

_____

APPLYING THE MESSAGE

13. What caused you to respond to the message of the gospel and receive the transforming power of the Holy Spirit in your life?

_____

_____

_____

_____

_____

_____

_____

14. How can you, like Peter, present the gospel message in a way that will open others to the transforming power of the Holy Spirit?

_____

_____

_____

_____

_____

_____

_____

_____

REFLECTING ON THE MEANING

On more than one occasion in the Bible, the filling of the Holy Spirit is mistaken for drunkenness. It is understandable. When people are drunk, they are no longer in control. They usually speak louder than they normally would and say and do things they would never typically say or do. When the Holy Spirit fills our lives as believers, the same thing happens—but in a good way. We begin to act supernaturally. We say and do godly things because we are empowered and controlled by the Spirit of God.

This should be the goal of everyone who is a Christian. We should desire that the Holy Spirit—who was poured out on the Day of Pentecost and is now living in our hearts—would be the controlling influence in our lives. Our prayer should be the same as Jesus spoke over His followers just before He left the earth:

> You shall receive power when the Holy Spirit has come upon you; and you shall be witnesses to Me in Jerusalem, and in all Judea and Samaria, and to the end of the earth (Acts 1:8).

God wants to work in our lives—to give us power and authority to boldly proclaim the message of the gospel. But we need to be willing for Him to work through us and use us as instruments of His grace. We must be open to saying, "Lord God, fill me. Control me with Your Spirit." Furthermore, we cannot do this in a false way. We cannot say, "Lord, control me," if we know in our hearts there is something we want to hang on to for ourselves. We have to totally release whatever it is to the Lord and say, "Lord God, I'm Yours. Come and fill me. Dictate everything that happens in my life. Make me sensitive to Your voice today. If someone comes across my path and I'm supposed to talk to them, tell me, and I'll do it."

When we do this, we can expect an adventure! We may find ourselves doing things we never expected we would do—because God is *in* us and doing His work *through* us. This was the secret to the early church, and it's the secret to any church or individual that God uses.

JOURNALING YOUR RESPONSE

What role does the Holy Spirit play in your life? How are you surrendering control to Him?

LESSON *two*

SUFFERING IN JESUS' NAME

Acts 3:1–4:37

GETTING STARTED

How do you typically respond when you encounter trials and difficulties in your life?

_____

_____

_____

_____

_____

_____

_____

_____

_____

_____

_____

_____

_____

_____

_____

_____

SETTING THE STAGE

If you have read the New Testament even casually, you know that God never promises that believers in Christ will go through this life pain-free and without encountering difficulties. Whenever you hear someone suggest the opposite, you can know that person hasn't read the Bible carefully! In reality, the New Testament provides a constant warning that believers *will* encounter suffering and persecution as part of their experience of walking with God.

Jesus told His disciples, "If the world hates you, you know that it hated Me before it hated you. If you were of the world, the world would love its own. Yet because you are not of the world, but I chose you out of the world, therefore the world hates you. Remember the word that I said to you, 'A servant is not greater than his master.' If they persecuted Me, they will also persecute you. If they kept My word, they will keep yours also" (John 15:18–20). The apostle Paul wrote, "All who desire to live godly in Christ Jesus will suffer persecution" (2 Timothy 3:12). And Peter wrote, "For to this you were called, because Christ also suffered for us, leaving us an example, that you should follow His steps" (1 Peter 2:21).

Given this, it should be no surprise that after Peter's sermon on the Day of Pentecost—when 3,000 people were added to the church on a single day—the persecution of this new movement would soon follow. The believers were gathering together, sharing their resources, proclaiming the gospel of Christ, and witnessing many signs and miracles taking place among them. All of this quickly got the attention of the Jewish religious elite—and they wanted to put a stop to this new movement before it could spread even further.

We should likewise not be surprised when we go through difficulties, trials, pain, and suffering. Of course, this is not a pleasant idea—for while most of us desire to follow Jesus' example of loving and serving others, none of us as are keen on following the example of the Lord in experiencing suffering and persecution. However, as we will see in this next section of Acts, this is just the common lot of those who follow the Lord.

EXPLORING THE TEXT

A Lame Man Healed (Acts 3:1–10)

---

[1] Now Peter and John went up together to the temple at the hour of prayer, the ninth hour. [2] And a certain man lame from his mother's womb was carried, whom they laid daily at the gate of the temple which is called Beautiful, to ask alms from those who entered the temple; [3] who, seeing Peter and John about to go into the temple, asked for alms. [4] And fixing his eyes on him, with John, Peter said, "Look at us." [5] So he gave them his attention, expecting to receive something from them. [6] Then Peter said, "Silver and gold I do not have, but what I do have I give you: In the name of Jesus Christ of Nazareth, rise up and walk." [7] And he took him by the right hand and lifted him up, and immediately his feet and ankle bones received strength. [8] So he, leaping up, stood and walked and entered the temple with them—walking, leaping, and praising God. [9] And all the people saw him walking and praising God. [10] Then they knew that it was he who sat begging alms at the Beautiful Gate of the temple; and they were filled with wonder and amazement at what had happened to him.

---

1. What did the man who was begging at the Beautiful Gate expect to receive from Peter and John? What did Peter offer to him instead (see verses 3–6)?

_____

_____

_____

_____

_____

2. How did the man respond when he was healed? How did the people respond when they saw that this man could now walk (see verses 8–10)?

_____

_____

_____

_____

Peter and John Arrested (Acts 4:1–12)

¹ Now as they spoke to the people, the priests, the captain of the temple, and the Sadducees came upon them, ² being greatly disturbed that they taught the people and preached in Jesus the resurrection from the dead. ³ And they laid hands on them, and put them in custody until the next day, for it was already evening. ⁴ However, many of those who heard the word believed; and the number of the men came to be about five thousand.

⁵ And it came to pass, on the next day, that their rulers, elders, and scribes, ⁶ as well as Annas the high priest, Caiaphas, John, and Alexander, and as many as were of the family of the high priest, were gathered together at Jerusalem. ⁷ And when they had set them in the midst, they asked, "By what power or by what name have you done this?"

⁸ Then Peter, filled with the Holy Spirit, said to them, "Rulers of the people and elders of Israel: ⁹ If we this day are judged for a good deed done to a helpless man, by what means he has been made well, ¹⁰ let it be known to you all, and to all the people of Israel, that by the name of Jesus Christ of Nazareth, whom you crucified, whom God raised from the dead, by Him this man stands here before you whole. ¹¹ This is the 'stone which was rejected by you builders, which has become the chief cornerstone.' ¹² Nor is there salvation in any other, for there is no other name under heaven given among men by which we must be saved."

3. After the man at the Beautiful Gate was healed, Peter delivered another sermon in which he proclaimed that Jesus was the Messiah whom God had raised from the dead (see Acts 2:11–26). How did the religious leaders—the priests, captain of the temple, and Sadducees—respond to Peter and John's actions? How did others respond (see verses 1–4)?

_____

_____

_____

_____

_____

_____

4. What did Peter say when the Jewish religious leaders asked "by what power" he and John had healed the man born lame? What did he say about Christ (see verses 9–12)?

_____

_____

_____

_____

_____

Peter and John Before the Sanhedrin (Acts 4:13–22)

¹³ Now when they saw the boldness of Peter and John, and perceived that they were uneducated and untrained men, they marveled. And they realized that they had been with Jesus. ¹⁴ And seeing the man who had been healed standing with them, they could say nothing against it. ¹⁵ But when they had commanded them to go aside out of the council, they conferred among themselves, ¹⁶ saying, "What shall we do to these men? For, indeed, that a notable miracle has been

done through them is evident to all who dwell in Jerusalem, and we cannot deny it. ¹⁷ But so that it spreads no further among the people, let us severely threaten them, that from now on they speak to no man in this name."

¹⁸ So they called them and commanded them not to speak at all nor teach in the name of Jesus. ¹⁹ But Peter and John answered and said to them, "Whether it is right in the sight of God to listen to you more than to God, you judge. ²⁰ For we cannot but speak the things which we have seen and heard." ²¹ So when they had further threatened them, they let them go, finding no way of punishing them, because of the people, since they all glorified God for what had been done. ²² For the man was over forty years old on whom this miracle of healing had been performed.

---

5. Why did the Jewish religious leaders marvel at the words and boldness of Peter and John? What were they most concerned about as it related to this miracle (see verses 13–17)?

_____

_____

_____

_____

_____

6. How did Peter and John reply to the council's command not to speak or teach in the name of Jesus (see verses 19–20)?

_____

_____

_____

_____

_____

The Believers Pray (Acts 4:23–37)

[23] And being let go, they went to their own companions and reported all that the chief priests and elders had said to them. [24] So when they heard that, they raised their voice to God with one accord and said: "Lord, You are God, who made heaven and earth and the sea, and all that is in them, [25] who by the mouth of Your servant David have said:

'Why did the nations rage,
And the people plot vain things?
[26] The kings of the earth took their stand,
And the rulers were gathered together
Against the LORD and against His Christ.'

[27] "For truly against Your holy Servant Jesus, whom You anointed, both Herod and Pontius Pilate, with the Gentiles and the people of Israel, were gathered together [28] to do whatever Your hand and Your purpose determined before to be done. [29] Now, Lord, look on their threats, and grant to Your servants that with all boldness they may speak Your word, [30] by stretching out Your hand to heal, and that signs and wonders may be done through the name of Your holy Servant Jesus."

[31] And when they had prayed, the place where they were assembled together was shaken; and they were all filled with the Holy Spirit, and they spoke the word of God with boldness.

[32] Now the multitude of those who believed were of one heart and one soul; neither did anyone say that any of the things he possessed was his own, but they had all things in common. [33] And with great power the apostles gave witness to the resurrection of the Lord Jesus. And great grace was upon them all. [34] Nor was there anyone among them who lacked; for all who were possessors of lands or houses sold them, and brought the proceeds of the things that were

sold, [35] and laid them at the apostles' feet; and they distributed to each as anyone had need.

[36] And Joses, who was also named Barnabas by the apostles (which is translated Son of Encouragement), a Levite of the country of Cyprus, [37] having land, sold it, and brought the money and laid it at the apostles' feet.

---

7. For what did the believers pray after they learned Peter and John had been threatened and told not to preach the gospel (see verses 29–30)?

_____

_____

_____

_____

_____

_____

_____

8. How did the believers in Christ treat one another after this event? What came to characterize this true fellowship of believers (see verses 32–35)?

_____

_____

_____

_____

_____

_____

REVIEWING THE STORY

When Peter and John encountered a man who been born lame, they commanded him in the name of Jesus to rise up and walk—and he immediately started leaping and praising God. The miracle occurred at the Beautiful Gate in the Temple, and those who witnessed the miracle were filled with wonder and amazement. The Jewish religious leaders, alarmed by the news, quickly arrested Peter and John. When Peter was given a chance to speak, he delivered a powerful sermon that stunned the council. They had no way to respond to his words, so they simply ordered the apostles not to preach the gospel anymore. Peter and John replied they could not help but talk about what they had seen Jesus do and heard Him say. Just as they were willing to preach and heal in Jesus' name, they were willing to boldly suffer in His name.

9. How did Peter respond to the beggar's request for money (see Acts 3:5–6)?

10. What question did the Jewish religious leaders ask that set the stage for Peter's epic response (see Acts 4:7)?

11. What dilemma did the accusers of Peter and John face
(see Acts 4:14–17)?

_____

_____

_____

_____

_____

_____

12. What happened after the believers prayed for boldness to carry out
God's work in spite of the threats of the Jewish officials (see Acts 4:31)?

_____

_____

_____

_____

_____

_____

APPLYING THE MESSAGE

13. What might be some ways that God is calling you and the people
of your church to act in boldness in your own community?

_____

_____

_____

_____

_____

14. What steps can you take to serve others like the members did in the early church?

_____

_____

_____

_____

_____

_____

_____

_____

_____

REFLECTING ON THE MEANING

When Peter and John told their fellow believers about their experience at the Temple—including their arrest—they rejoiced that the persecution had opened up the way for the apostles to preach the gospel before the Sanhedrin. The believers proclaimed, "Lord, You are God, who made heaven and earth and the sea" (Acts 4:24). In this praise, they used a Greek term for God from which we get the word *despot*, referring to a master who is in total control. They were confident the God to whom they prayed was the God who was in control!

Notice that these believers didn't pray for *safety*. They didn't pray for *asylum*. They didn't even pray for *protection* from the enemies of the gospel. Rather, they prayed that their sovereign Lord would give them even greater *boldness* (see Acts 4:29–30). They asked Him to help them do what the Sanhedrin had forbidden them to do—speak and teach in the name of Christ. They petitioned God to continue to work healings, signs, and wonders in the people's midst through the name of Jesus.

God heard the prayer of His servants, and they were filled with the Holy Spirit. The first persecution had come to the early church, but instead of being defeated by it, the believers became bolder and stronger in their faith. They became more aggressive in their outreach. In the same way,

God may use times of suffering and trials to cause us to grow. If we stay focused and pray, as those believers did in the early church, we will also see God's blessing on us.

JOURNALING YOUR RESPONSE

What might happen if you prayed for more boldness in sharing the gospel?

COMPLETE COMMITMENT

Acts 5:1–6:15

GETTING STARTED

How can you tell if someone's Christian commitment is sincere?

_____

_____

_____

_____

_____

_____

_____

_____

_____

_____

_____

_____

_____

SETTING THE STAGE

In the book of Acts, we read amazing stories of the miraculous works the Holy Spirit was doing in and through the members of the early church.

God had chosen to place His presence—His very Spirit—within the believers and was at work in their midst. He had called them to lead holy lives and faithfully follow the teachings of Jesus. As a result, the church was growing larger each day . . . yet the believers still experienced trials and conflicts that tested their faith.

In this next section in Acts, we read of one of these trials involving a couple named Ananias and Sapphira. The trouble began when this husband and wife learned that Barnabas had sold a piece of land and "brought the money and laid it at the apostles' feet" (4:37). They wanted to be recognized for doing the same . . . but they were not willing to completely commit to the cause. So, instead, they held back some of the money for themselves.

What happens next is one of most difficult accounts in all of Acts for believers and non-believers alike to comprehend. Many have questioned why Ananias and Sapphira were judged so swiftly for their lies rather than given the opportunity to repent. Many have scrutinized Peter's ethics in the matter and found him to be without compassion or restraint in this story. Others have found it difficult to understand why any leader of the early church would have shown such harshness for such a "slight" matter.

However, we have to remember that God is holy *and* just. In the Old Testament, we read of many examples of His immediate judgment against disobedience (see, for example, 2 Samuel 6:6–9, Leviticus 10, Joshua 7, and 2 Chronicles 26:16–21). These stories are not any more comfortable than the account of Ananias and Sapphira, but they do reveal that we can't have both sin and holiness in our lives. Life as a member of the body of Christ requires *complete* commitment to the living God. It cannot be taken lightly.

EXPLORING THE TEXT

Lying to the Holy Spirit (Acts 5:1–11)

---

¹ But a certain man named Ananias, with Sapphira his wife, sold a possession. ² And he kept back part of the proceeds, his wife also being aware of it, and brought a certain part and laid it at the

apostles' feet. ³ But Peter said, "Ananias, why has Satan filled your heart to lie to the Holy Spirit and keep back part of the price of the land for yourself? ⁴ While it remained, was it not your own? And after it was sold, was it not in your own control? Why have you conceived this thing in your heart? You have not lied to men but to God."

⁵ Then Ananias, hearing these words, fell down and breathed his last. So great fear came upon all those who heard these things. ⁶ And the young men arose and wrapped him up, carried him out, and buried him.

⁷ Now it was about three hours later when his wife came in, not knowing what had happened. ⁸ And Peter answered her, "Tell me whether you sold the land for so much?"

She said, "Yes, for so much."

⁹ Then Peter said to her, "How is it that you have agreed together to test the Spirit of the Lord? Look, the feet of those who have buried your husband are at the door, and they will carry you out." ¹⁰ Then immediately she fell down at his feet and breathed her last. And the young men came in and found her dead, and carrying her out, buried her by her husband. ¹¹ So great fear came upon all the church and upon all who heard these things.

---

1. What did Ananias and Sapphira do wrong? What did Peter say to Ananias about the act he and his wife had committed (see verses 1–4)?

_____

_____

_____

_____

_____

_____

_____

_____

2. What did Peter say to Sapphira when she lied? How did the church respond to these events that had occurred (see verses 9–11)?

_____

_____

_____

_____

_____

The Apostles on Trial (Acts 5:26–42)

26 Then the captain went with the officers and brought them without violence, for they feared the people, lest they should be stoned. 27 And when they had brought them, they set them before the council. And the high priest asked them, 28 saying, "Did we not strictly command you not to teach in this name? And look, you have filled Jerusalem with your doctrine, and intend to bring this Man's blood on us!"

29 But Peter and the other apostles answered and said: "We ought to obey God rather than men. 30 The God of our fathers raised up Jesus whom you murdered by hanging on a tree. 31 Him God has exalted to His right hand to be Prince and Savior, to give repentance to Israel and forgiveness of sins. 32 And we are His witnesses to these things, and so also is the Holy Spirit whom God has given to those who obey Him."

33 When they heard this, they were furious and plotted to kill them. 34 Then one in the council stood up, a Pharisee named Gamaliel, a teacher of the law held in respect by all the people, and commanded them to put the apostles outside for a little while. 35 And he said to them: "Men of Israel, take heed to yourselves what you intend to do regarding these men. 36 For some time ago Theudas rose up, claiming to be somebody. A number of men, about four hundred, joined him. He was slain, and all who obeyed him were scattered and came to nothing. 37 After this man, Judas of Galilee rose up in the days of the census, and drew away many people after him. He also perished, and

all who obeyed him were dispersed. [38] And now I say to you, keep away from these men and let them alone; for if this plan or this work is of men, it will come to nothing; [39] but if it is of God, you cannot overthrow it—lest you even be found to fight against God."

[40] And they agreed with him, and when they had called for the apostles and beaten them, they commanded that they should not speak in the name of Jesus, and let them go. [41] So they departed from the presence of the council, rejoicing that they were counted worthy to suffer shame for His name. [42] And daily in the temple, and in every house, they did not cease teaching and preaching Jesus as the Christ.

---

3. After the sad events of Ananias and Sapphira, the early church continued to grow—and continued to be a concern for the Jewish leaders. The Sadducees finally threw some of the apostles in jail, but they were freed by an angel that night and were back in the temple the next day to proclaim the gospel. What did the high priest say to them? How did Peter and the other apostles respond to this demand (see verses 28–32)?

_____

_____

_____

_____

_____

4. What advice did Gamaliel give to the council? Why do you think this persuaded the Jewish leaders to just beat the apostles instead of putting them to death (see verses 35–40)?

_____

_____

_____

_____

Seven Chosen to Serve (Acts 6:1–7)

¹ Now in those days, when the number of the disciples was multiply-
ing, there arose a complaint against the Hebrews by the Hellenists,
because their widows were neglected in the daily distribution.
² Then the twelve summoned the multitude of the disciples and said,
"It is not desirable that we should leave the word of God and serve
tables. ³ Therefore, brethren, seek out from among you seven men of
good reputation, full of the Holy Spirit and wisdom, whom we may
appoint over this business; ⁴ but we will give ourselves continually
to prayer and to the ministry of the word."

⁵ And the saying pleased the whole multitude. And they chose
Stephen, a man full of faith and the Holy Spirit, and Philip, Prochorus,
Nicanor, Timon, Parmenas, and Nicolas, a proselyte from Antioch,
⁶ whom they set before the apostles; and when they had prayed,
they laid hands on them.

⁷ Then the word of God spread, and the number of the disciples
multiplied greatly in Jerusalem, and a great many of the priests were
obedient to the faith.

5. Most scholars identify the Hellenists as a group of Greek-speaking
Jews who had been dispersed to other lands by foreign powers and had
returned to Israel. The Jewish elite tended to look down on these "Greek
Jews," and some of these attitudes were evidently carried into the early
church. What was the source of the Hellenists' complaint (see verse 1)?

6. How did the apostles decide to address the issue? What types of responsibilities did they choose to delegate so they could focus on preaching the gospel (see verses 2–4)?

_____

_____

_____

_____

_____

_____

_____

_____

_____

_____

_____

Stephen Accused of Blasphemy (Acts 6:8–15)

[8] And Stephen, full of faith and power, did great wonders and signs among the people. [9] Then there arose some from what is called the Synagogue of the Freedmen (Cyrenians, Alexandrians, and those from Cilicia and Asia), disputing with Stephen. [10] And they were not able to resist the wisdom and the Spirit by which he spoke. [11] Then they secretly induced men to say, "We have heard him speak blasphemous words against Moses and God." [12] And they stirred up the people, the elders, and the scribes; and they came upon him, seized him, and brought him to the council. [13] They also set up false witnesses who said, "This man does not cease to speak blasphemous words against this holy place and the law; [14] for we have heard him say that this Jesus of Nazareth will destroy this place and change the customs which Moses delivered to us." [15] And all who sat in the council, looking steadfastly at him, saw his face as the face of an angel.

7. Stephen was one of the men chosen to minister to the Greek-speaking believers, which brought him into conflict with a group within the Hellenistic Jews called the "Synagogue of the Freedmen." What caused Stephen to end up at odds with this group (see verses 9–10)?

_____

_____

_____

_____

_____

_____

_____

8. What tactics did the Freedmen use to stir up the people, the elders, and the scribes? What happened as a result (see verses 11–12)?

_____

_____

_____

_____

_____

_____

_____

REVIEWING THE STORY

The early church faced a number of trials and growing pains. Perhaps the first true test of its endurance came when a couple named Ananias and Sapphira sold a piece of land and lied about giving all the proceeds to the church. Their plan to make themselves look generous backfired and they were struck dead for lying to the Holy Spirit. Later, Peter and the apostles were arrested for healing a multitude of sick people, but an angel set them free. Their recapture set the stage for a trial in front of the Jewish religious authorities. They were beaten and commanded to never again preach the gospel, but they remained firmly committed to Christ and ignored the command. Another issue within the church arose when the Hellenist believers accused the Hebrew believers of not caring for Hellenist widows. The apostles chose seven men to handle the situation and manage other difficult situations. One of them, Stephen, was targeted by the Jewish leaders and soon put on trial for blasphemy against God.

9. What did Peter say was the real issue that had caused the Lord to immediately strike down Ananias and Sapphira for their sin (see Acts 5:3, 9)?

10. What instruction did the angel give the apostles after he set them free (see Acts 5:20)?

11. What happened after the apostles appointed seven men to take care of the day-to-day issues within the church (see Acts 6:7)?

_____

_____

_____

_____

_____

_____

12. How did Stephen come to the attention of the Synagogue of the Freedmen (see Acts 6:8)?

_____

_____

_____

_____

_____

APPLYING THE MESSAGE

13. How were the apostles able to rejoice after they had been beaten and threatened for sharing their Christian faith?

_____

_____

_____

_____

_____

_____

14. How can you become bolder in your Christian faith?

_____

_____

_____

_____

_____

_____

_____

_____

REFLECTING ON THE MEANING

The story of Ananias and Sapphira teaches us about the gravity of sin. Some people wonder why God punished them in such an extreme manner. The answer may lie in the fact that something new—something *essential*—was being established. God wanted His people to understand the importance of purity in His relationship with them. As the persecution of the early church reveals, our walk of faith is not a part-time commitment or something to be taken lightly. God is looking for fully committed people to do His work on this earth.

Satan's strategy is to cause discord, divisiveness, deceit, and insincerity among God's people. If his strategy had been successful in the early church, it would have resulted in a much different story than the one we read in the book of Acts. Thankfully, God intervened in the story of Ananias and Sapphira and elsewhere—and both His judgment and mercy served as an example to the believers of the seriousness of their commitment to Him.

God was making a statement in the book of Acts that still resonates today. His people listened, and the early church continued to grow in spite of the many problems its members faced. We can learn a vital lesson from their experiences: neither persecution from without nor pressures from within can defeat a church that is populated by Spirit-filled believers who honor God and respect His holy Word.

JOURNALING YOUR RESPONSE

How can you keep Satan from gaining a foothold in your circle of influence in your church?

PERSECUTION AND TRIALS

Acts 7:1–8:40

GETTING STARTED

If you were to stand trial for being a Christian, what evidence could be used against you?

_____

_____

_____

_____

_____

_____

_____

_____

_____

_____

_____

SETTING THE STAGE

Stephen had been chosen by the disciples as one of "seven men of good reputation" (Acts 6:3) to serve in the early church. But a group called the Synagogue of the Freedmen had risen up against Stephen and compelled the religious leaders to put him on trial. They found false witnesses to accuse him of blasphemy against God, against Moses, against the law, and against the Jewish temple. At one point, the high priest asks Stephen, "Are these things so?" (7:1). The rest of Acts 7 is built around Stephen's response to the four charges against him.

What follows is not traditional courtroom procedure on Stephen's part—and for good reason. He is not hoping to be acquitted. In fact, he knows he is *not* going to be acquitted. Even more, he knows it is highly likely he is going to be put to death for what he is about to say. But Stephen is not interested in offering a defense of himself. Instead, he wants to seize the opportunity to offer a defense of Christianity. Furthermore, he knows the Jewish leaders pride themselves on their knowledge of the Old Testament, so he uses that text and goes back to the beginning of their history as a people to show them Christ throughout the Old Testament.

Stephen obviously had no time to prepare sermon notes or even think much about the logical progression of his defense. Yet as he stands in front of the Jewish scholars, an epic sermon pours out of his mouth. This was a man who was anointed by the Spirit of God as a preacher—a deacon whom God promoted to be an evangelist. The Bible records only this single sermon by Stephen, but it is a sermon that has forever shaped the Christian church.

The story of Stephen also introduces us to another character who will play a major role not only in the book of Acts but also in the rest of church history. For watching the events that day was a Pharisee named Saul . . . whom we know today as Paul. But before he would become the great apostle to the Gentiles, he would first be a great persecutor of the early church.

EXPLORING THE TEXT

Stephen's Great Sermon (Acts 7:37–53)

37 "This is that Moses who said to the children of Israel, 'The LORD your God will raise up for you a Prophet like me from your brethren. Him you shall hear.'

[38] "This is he who was in the congregation in the wilderness with the Angel who spoke to him on Mount Sinai, and with our fathers, the one who received the living oracles to give to us, [39] whom our fathers would not obey, but rejected. And in their hearts they turned back to Egypt, [40] saying to Aaron, 'Make us gods to go before us; as for this Moses who brought us out of the land of Egypt, we do not know what has become of him.' [41] And they made a calf in those days, offered sacrifices to the idol, and rejoiced in the works of their own hands. [42] Then God turned and gave them up to worship the host of heaven, as it is written in the book of the Prophets:

'Did you offer Me slaughtered animals and sacrifices during forty
   years in the wilderness,
O house of Israel?
[43] You also took up the tabernacle of Moloch,
And the star of your god Remphan,
Images which you made to worship;
And I will carry you away beyond Babylon.'

[44] "Our fathers had the tabernacle of witness in the wilderness, as He appointed, instructing Moses to make it according to the pattern that he had seen, [45] which our fathers, having received it in turn, also brought with Joshua into the land possessed by the Gentiles, whom God drove out before the face of our fathers until the days of David, [46] who found favor before God and asked to find a dwelling for the God of Jacob. [47] But Solomon built Him a house.
[48] "However, the Most High does not dwell in temples made with hands, as the prophet says:

[49] 'Heaven is My throne,
And earth is My footstool.
What house will you build for Me? says the LORD,
Or what is the place of My rest?
[50] Has My hand not made all these things?'

⁵¹ "You stiff-necked and uncircumcised in heart and ears! You always resist the Holy Spirit; as your fathers did, so do you. ⁵² Which of the prophets did your fathers not persecute? And they killed those who foretold the coming of the Just One, of whom you now have become the betrayers and murderers, ⁵³ who have received the law by the direction of angels and have not kept it."

---

1. Stephen's defense is a pronouncement of Jesus as the Jewish Messiah and a condemnation of the religious leaders for rejecting Him. How does Stephen draw on the story of Moses to show how God was pointing His people to a greater Prophet to come? How did Stephen show the Israelites had a history of rejecting their prophets (see verses 37–40)?

_____

_____

_____

_____

2. What accusations did Stephen finally raise against the religious leaders? In what ways had they (and their forefathers) resisted the Holy Spirit (see verses 51–53)?

_____

_____

_____

_____

Stephen's Execution (Acts 7:54–60)

⁵⁴ When they heard these things they were cut to the heart, and they gnashed at him with their teeth. ⁵⁵ But he, being full of the Holy Spirit, gazed into heaven and saw the glory of God, and Jesus standing at the right hand of God, ⁵⁶ and said, "Look! I see the heavens opened and the Son of Man standing at the right hand of God!"

> [57] Then they cried out with a loud voice, stopped their ears, and ran at him with one accord; [58] and they cast him out of the city and stoned him. And the witnesses laid down their clothes at the feet of a young man named Saul. [59] And they stoned Stephen as he was calling on God and saying, "Lord Jesus, receive my spirit." [60] Then he knelt down and cried out with a loud voice, "Lord, do not charge them with this sin." And when he had said this, he fell asleep.

3. Luke uses the phrase "gnashed . . . their teeth" to show the anger the Jewish leaders felt toward Stephen. This only intensified when Stephen said he saw Jesus standing at the right hand of God. Why would this cause such fury in the religious leaders (see verses 54–57)?

_____

_____

_____

4. Jesus prayed a similar prayer for His executioners as He was dying on the cross (see Luke 34:34). How did Stephen follow the example of Jesus, his Master, even in his final moments (see Acts 7:59–60)?

_____

_____

_____

_____

Persecution and Scattering (Acts 8:1–8)

> [1] Now Saul was consenting to his death.
>
> At that time a great persecution arose against the church which was at Jerusalem; and they were all scattered throughout the regions of Judea and Samaria, except the apostles. [2] And devout men carried Stephen to his burial, and made great lamentation over him.

³ As for Saul, he made havoc of the church, entering every house, and dragging off men and women, committing them to prison.

⁴ Therefore those who were scattered went everywhere preaching the word. ⁵ Then Philip went down to the city of Samaria and preached Christ to them. ⁶ And the multitudes with one accord heeded the things spoken by Philip, hearing and seeing the miracles which he did. ⁷ For unclean spirits, crying with a loud voice, came out of many who were possessed; and many who were paralyzed and lame were healed. ⁸ And there was great joy in that city.

5. Paul would later write, "You have heard of my former conduct in Judaism, how I persecuted the church of God beyond measure and tried to destroy it" (Galatians 1:13). How did Paul persecute the early church? What was his motivation for doing so (see Acts 8:1–3)?

6. The persecution of the church that broke out after Stephen's execution served to scatter the apostles to different places. Where did Philip, another of the "seven men of good reputation" (Acts 6:3), go to preach the gospel? What was the result (see 8:5–8)?

Philip and the Ethiopian (Acts 8:26–40)

²⁶ Now an angel of the Lord spoke to Philip, saying, "Arise and go toward the south along the road which goes down from Jerusalem to Gaza." This is desert. ²⁷ So he arose and went. And behold, a man of Ethiopia, a eunuch of great authority under Candace the queen of the Ethiopians, who had charge of all her treasury, and had come to Jerusalem to worship, ²⁸ was returning. And sitting in his chariot, he was reading Isaiah the prophet. ²⁹ Then the Spirit said to Philip, "Go near and overtake this chariot."

³⁰ So Philip ran to him, and heard him reading the prophet Isaiah, and said, "Do you understand what you are reading?"

³¹ And he said, "How can I, unless someone guides me?" And he asked Philip to come up and sit with him. ³² The place in the Scripture which he read was this:

"He was led as a sheep to the slaughter;
And as a lamb before its shearer is silent,
So He opened not His mouth.
³³ In His humiliation His justice was taken away,
And who will declare His generation?
For His life is taken from the earth."

³⁴ So the eunuch answered Philip and said, "I ask you, of whom does the prophet say this, of himself or of some other man?" ³⁵ Then Philip opened his mouth, and beginning at this Scripture, preached Jesus to him. ³⁶ Now as they went down the road, they came to some water. And the eunuch said, "See, here is water. What hinders me from being baptized?"

³⁷ Then Philip said, "If you believe with all your heart, you may."

And he answered and said, "I believe that Jesus Christ is the Son of God."

³⁸ So he commanded the chariot to stand still. And both Philip and the eunuch went down into the water, and he baptized him. ³⁹ Now

when they came up out of the water, the Spirit of the Lord caught Philip away, so that the eunuch saw him no more; and he went on his way rejoicing. [40] But Philip was found at Azotus. And passing through, he preached in all the cities till he came to Caesarea.

___

7. How did God use the persecutions in Israel to spread the message of Christ? What part did Philip play in this (see verses 26–29)?

_____

_____

_____

_____

_____

_____

8. What did the Ethiopian official want Philip to explain to him? How did Philip respond to his question (see verses 31–35)?

_____

_____

_____

_____

_____

_____

Reviewing the Story

Stephen used his trial before the Jewish leaders to deliver a sermon that traced the redemptive work of Jesus throughout the Old Testament. His words sent the Jewish leaders into a frenzy, and they killed him. One of the witnesses to Stephen's death was Saul (later known as Paul), and he took part in a great persecution that scattered the believers throughout the region. Philip, one of the seven chosen by the disciples, preached Christ in Samaria and witnessed many come to salvation. Following this, the Holy Spirit directed him to an official of Ethiopia, where he revealed how Jesus was the promised Messiah prophesied in the Old Testament.

9. How did Stephen end his sermon to the Jewish religious leaders (see Acts 7:51–53)?

_____

_____

_____

_____

_____

10. What did Stephen witness as his accusers were putting him to death (see Acts 7:55–56)?

_____

_____

_____

_____

_____

11. What did Saul do after he gave his consent to Stephen's death (see Acts 8:3)?

_____

_____

_____

_____

_____

12. How did Philip help the Ethiopian official realize that Jesus was the Messiah whom had been promised in the Old Testament (see Acts 8:30–35)?

_____

_____

_____

_____

_____

_____

APPLYING THE MESSAGE

13. When was a time you were put on the spot because of your faith? What lessons did you take away from the experience?

_____

_____

_____

_____

_____

_____

_____

14. How have you seen God use challenges and trials to further the work of His kingdom?

_____

_____

_____

_____

_____

_____

REFLECTING ON THE MEANING

The authors of the New Testament frequently depicted Jesus sitting at the right hand of God. The apostle Paul wrote that God "raised [Jesus] from the dead and seated Him at His right hand in the heavenly places" (Ephesians 1:20; see also Romans 8:34 and Colossians 3:1). The author of Hebrews wrote Jesus, "when He had by Himself purged our sins, sat down at the right hand of the Majesty on high" (Hebrews 1:3). However, when Stephen was given a glimpse into the heavenly throne room at his execution, he saw something different.

Luke tells us that as Stephen was being put to death, he exclaimed, "Look! I see the heavens opened and the Son of Man standing at the right hand of God!" (Acts 7:56). Jesus was *standing*. He had risen to His feet. The image presented in Luke's account is one of Jesus welcoming home a loyal servant. Stephen had proved himself faithful unto death, so Jesus rose to welcome him into eternal life.

Most Christians aspire to be as courageous as Stephen and boldly proclaim the gospel in any situation. We desire to be as courageous as Philip in his travels so the Lord can use us to further His work. We want to receive the welcome these men received from Jesus . . . and yet, in today's world, it is easier for us to want to camouflage our faith and live as underground Christians. We speak boldly on Sunday of the godly principles and priorities that matter to us—but then we speak timidly of them the rest of the week. We treat our Christian beliefs as an open secret outside of church. We are not ashamed of them, but neither are we making them known. In short, it's easy for us to be cowardly in our faith.

The stories of Stephen and Philip help us to understand that God has called us to a *courageous* faith. Our courage comes from our conviction, and our conviction comes from the Word of God. If we fix our hearts on God's Word, we will get conviction. When we get conviction, God will give us courage.

And when we have courage, we will do even the hard things that come our way for the sake of His kingdom.

JOURNALING YOUR RESPONSE

For what specific circumstances or situations in your life do you need conviction and courage?

THE HUNTER BECOMES THE HUNTED

Acts 9:1–43

GETTING STARTED

What is the most dramatic story you have heard of how a person came to believe in Christ?

_____

_____

_____

_____

_____

_____

_____

_____

_____

_____

_____

_____

_____

_____

_____

_____

_____

SETTING THE STAGE

As the events unfold in this next section of Acts, a man named Saul has been creating havoc in the early church. Luke tells us he has entered every house in Jerusalem, dragging off believers in Christ and committing them to prison (see Acts 8:3). But for Saul this is not enough, for he knows the persecutions have caused the believers to scatter. So, "still breathing threats and murder against the disciples of the Lord," (9:1), he decides to go to the high priest to get authorization to extend the persecutions to Damascus. What happens next on the road to that city changes not only Saul's life but also the course of human history.

For Luke, the conversion of Saul was the most important event in the early church. In fact, it was so important that he records it *three times* in the book of Acts. The story appears here in Acts 9:1–19, and it is found again in Acts 22:6–16 and Acts 26:12–18. The story occupies more space in the New Testament than any other with the exception of the events surrounding the crucifixion, burial, and resurrection of Jesus Christ. In other words, there is more coverage of Saul's conversion than of any other story except that of the Savior. Saul's conversion on the road to Damascus is indeed the pivot on which his life *and* the life of the church forever turned.

Perhaps it was fitting that Saul should experience such a unique conversion . . . for he was a unique person. He was a Jew by birth, a Roman by citizenship, a Greek by education, and a Christian by grace. Missionary and theologian, evangelist and pastor, organizer and leader, thinker and statesman—the many-sided man who later became known as Paul the apostle has influence that continues to this day to reach wide and deep.

EXPLORING THE TEXT

Saul Encounters the Risen Christ (Acts 9:1–9)

¹ Then Saul, still breathing threats and murder against the disciples of the Lord, went to the high priest ² and asked letters from him to the

synagogues of Damascus, so that if he found any who were of the Way, whether men or women, he might bring them bound to Jerusalem.

³ As he journeyed he came near Damascus, and suddenly a light shone around him from heaven. ⁴ Then he fell to the ground, and heard a voice saying to him, "Saul, Saul, why are you persecuting Me?"

⁵ And he said, "Who are You, Lord?"

Then the Lord said, "I am Jesus, whom you are persecuting. It is hard for you to kick against the goads."

⁶ So he, trembling and astonished, said, "Lord, what do You want me to do?"

Then the Lord said to him, "Arise and go into the city, and you will be told what you must do."

⁷ And the men who journeyed with him stood speechless, hearing a voice but seeing no one. ⁸ Then Saul arose from the ground, and when his eyes were opened he saw no one. But they led him by the hand and brought him into Damascus. ⁹ And he was three days without sight, and neither ate nor drank.

---

1. What do Saul's actions reveal about how he viewed the members of "the Way" (an early term used for followers of Christ) as a threat against the Jewish faith (see verses 1–2)?

_____

_____

_____

_____

2. What was the immediate aftermath of Saul's encounter with Jesus (see verses 8–9)?

_____

_____

_____

_____

Saul's Physical and Spiritual Healing (Acts 9:10–19)

¹⁰ Now there was a certain disciple at Damascus named Ananias; and to him the Lord said in a vision, "Ananias."

And he said, "Here I am, Lord."

¹¹ So the Lord said to him, "Arise and go to the street called Straight, and inquire at the house of Judas for one called Saul of Tarsus, for behold, he is praying. ¹² And in a vision he has seen a man named Ananias coming in and putting his hand on him, so that he might receive his sight."

¹³ Then Ananias answered, "Lord, I have heard from many about this man, how much harm he has done to Your saints in Jerusalem. ¹⁴ And here he has authority from the chief priests to bind all who call on Your name."

¹⁵ But the Lord said to him, "Go, for he is a chosen vessel of Mine to bear My name before Gentiles, kings, and the children of Israel. ¹⁶ For I will show him how many things he must suffer for My name's sake."

¹⁷ And Ananias went his way and entered the house; and laying his hands on him he said, "Brother Saul, the Lord Jesus, who appeared to you on the road as you came, has sent me that you may receive your sight and be filled with the Holy Spirit." ¹⁸ Immediately there fell from his eyes something like scales, and he received his sight at once; and he arose and was baptized.

¹⁹ So when he had received food, he was strengthened. Then Saul spent some days with the disciples at Damascus.

---

3. What did God instruct Ananias to do in the vision? Why was Ananias reluctant to follow these instructions (see verses 11–14)?

4. What had God appointed Saul to do? Why do you think He struck Paul with blindness and lead Ananias to him for healing (see verses 15–17)?

_____

_____

_____

_____

_____

_____

The Believers' Reaction to Saul (Acts 9:20–31)

[20] Immediately [Saul] preached the Christ in the synagogues, that He is the Son of God.

[21] Then all who heard were amazed, and said, "Is this not he who destroyed those who called on this name in Jerusalem, and has come here for that purpose, so that he might bring them bound to the chief priests?"

[22] But Saul increased all the more in strength, and confounded the Jews who dwelt in Damascus, proving that this Jesus is the Christ.

[23] Now after many days were past, the Jews plotted to kill him. [24] But their plot became known to Saul. And they watched the gates day and night, to kill him. [25] Then the disciples took him by night and let him down through the wall in a large basket.

[26] And when Saul had come to Jerusalem, he tried to join the disciples; but they were all afraid of him, and did not believe that he was a disciple. [27] But Barnabas took him and brought him to the apostles. And he declared to them how he had seen the Lord on the road, and that He had spoken to him, and how he had preached boldly at Damascus in the name of Jesus. [28] So he was with them at Jerusalem, coming in and going out. [29] And he spoke boldly in the name of the Lord Jesus and disputed against the Hellenists, but they attempted to kill him. [30] When the brethren found out, they brought him down to Caesarea and sent him out to Tarsus.

³¹ Then the churches throughout all Judea, Galilee, and Samaria had peace and were edified. And walking in the fear of the Lord and in the comfort of the Holy Spirit, they were multiplied.

---

5. Luke provides an overview of the events after Saul's conversion. It is likely Saul/Paul preached in the synagogues of Damascus for a time, went into Arabia (see Galatians 1:17), returned to Damascus, and then made his first visit to Jerusalem some three years after his conversion (see 1:18–24). Regardless, what was the situation that necessitated his hasty leave from the city of Damascus (see Acts 9:22–25)?

_____

_____

_____

_____

_____

6. It seems probable that stories had been in circulation about what evils against the church Saul had been doing in the three-year period after leaving Damascus. How might this have incited the events that transpired when he reached Jerusalem? What problems did Saul encounter with the Hellenists in the city (see verses 26–30)?

_____

_____

_____

_____

_____

Aeneas Healed (Acts 9:32–43)

³² Now it came to pass, as Peter went through all parts of the country, that he also came down to the saints who dwelt in Lydda. ³³ There he found a certain man named Aeneas, who had been bedridden

eight years and was paralyzed. ³⁴ And Peter said to him, "Aeneas, Jesus the Christ heals you. Arise and make your bed." Then he arose immediately. ³⁵ So all who dwelt at Lydda and Sharon saw him and turned to the Lord.

³⁶ At Joppa there was a certain disciple named Tabitha, which is translated Dorcas. This woman was full of good works and charitable deeds which she did. ³⁷ But it happened in those days that she became sick and died. When they had washed her, they laid her in an upper room. ³⁸ And since Lydda was near Joppa, and the disciples had heard that Peter was there, they sent two men to him, imploring him not to delay in coming to them. ³⁹ Then Peter arose and went with them. When he had come, they brought him to the upper room. And all the widows stood by him weeping, showing the tunics and garments which Dorcas had made while she was with them. ⁴⁰ But Peter put them all out, and knelt down and prayed. And turning to the body he said, "Tabitha, arise." And she opened her eyes, and when she saw Peter she sat up. ⁴⁰ Then he gave her his hand and lifted her up; and when he had called the saints and widows, he presented her alive. ⁴² And it became known throughout all Joppa, and many believed on the Lord. ⁴³ So it was that he stayed many days in Joppa with Simon, a tanner.

---

7. After relating the events of Saul's conversion, Luke shows the other apostles were also working to spread the gospel throughout the known world. The town of Lydda was located twenty-five miles northwest of Jerusalem. What effect did the healing of Aeneas have on the people in the region? How did this spread the gospel (see verses 34–35)?

8. The port city of Joppa was located ten miles northwest of Lydda. While it is not known what the believers there expected of Peter, it is telling they had washed but not yet *anointed* Tabitha's body for burial. What was the result of their faith? How did this event serve to further spread the good news of Christ to the world (see verses 37, 40–42)?

_____

_____

_____

_____

_____

_____

_____

_____

_____

_____

REVIEWING THE STORY

Saul wanted to expand his persecution of Christians and obtained authorization from the high priest to arrest believers in the city of Damascus. However, on the way there, he encountered the risen Christ and his life was forever changed. He was temporarily blinded, but God sent a disciple named Ananias to restore his sight. People were understandably suspicious when Saul began preaching the gospel, and some of his fellow persecutors tried to kill him. Saul was able to escape and fled to the surrounding area (known at the time as Arabia), where he remained for three years. He then went to Jerusalem, where the church leaders were afraid of him, but was welcomed by Barnabas. When another threat arose against his life, he fled to his home city of Tarsus. Meanwhile, Peter continued his own ministry of spreading the good news of Christ to the world by preaching and performing healings in Lydda and Joppa.

9. How did Jesus introduce Himself to Saul on the road to Damascus (see Acts 9:5)?

10. What did Ananias say when he found Saul? What happened when he prayed for Saul (see Acts 9:17–18)?

11. What impact did Saul's conversion have on the early church (see Acts 9:31)?

12. What was the result of the miracles God worked through Peter in the cities of Lydda and Joppa (see Acts 9:42)?

_____

_____

_____

_____

_____

APPLYING THE MESSAGE

13. What does Saul's story teach about the kinds of people whom God uses for His work?

_____

_____

_____

_____

_____

_____

14. When have you been tempted to write off someone as "too far gone"? When have you been tempted to believe that you are "too far gone" to be used by God?

_____

_____

_____

_____

_____

REFLECTING ON THE MEANING

Luke first introduces us to the man who would become known as the apostle Paul at the end of his story of the execution of Stephen (see Acts 7:58). We go on to read that Paul was "consenting to his death" and sought to create "havoc of the church" (8:1, 3). Luke then tells us about Paul's dramatic conversion on the road to Damascus . . . and much of the rest of Acts will focus on his work among the Gentiles. But Luke is careful to note that Paul was not the only minister of the gospel. The disciple Peter was also greatly involved in spreading the message of Christ. Like Paul, he also traveled from place to place, starting in Lydda and Joppa.

The stories of Peter and Paul reveal that God often uses the most *unlikely of people* to carry out His purposes in the world. Peter, an uneducated fisherman, was the disciple who three times denied even knowing Christ. Paul, a well-educated Pharisee, was so zealous in his defense of his Jewish faith that he tried to put an end to Christianity. Both stories reveal the transforming power that Jesus can make in a life—and they also reveal that God uses *busy people* to grow His kingdom. In fact, throughout Christian history, we find the people God has called moving constantly through their world to do the work that He has given them to do. They do not sit around waiting for something to do. They busy themselves doing something . . . and in the midst of their doing, God calls them to do something else.

The best way to find God's will is to busy yourself doing the things He has already revealed to you. The question is not, "What does God *ultimately* want me to do?" but, "What does God want me to do *today*?" You will discover the answer to that question when you become actively involved in serving Him—whether that is teaching, preaching, or some other act. Your responsibility is simply to do what you can do with what God has provided for you.

When you do this, God will lead you into new areas, and His blessing will abide in you.

Journaling Your Response

What needs to change in your life for you to always be available for God's use?

_____

_____

_____

_____

_____

_____

_____

_____

_____

_____

_____

_____

_____

_____

_____

_____

_____

_____

_____

_____

_____

_____

_____

_____

_____

_____

_____

THE GOSPEL COMES TO THE GENTILES

Acts 10:1–11:30

GETTING STARTED

What do you feel makes Christians reluctant to share the gospel with certain people today?

_____

_____

_____

_____

_____

_____

_____

_____

_____

_____

_____

_____

SETTING THE STAGE

It's no secret the Jewish people wanted little to do with non-Jewish people . . . a group the New Testament refers to as the "Gentiles." In that time, Jews would not enter as guests into any Gentile home. They considered dirt from a Gentile country as defiled, so they would shake it off their sandals before walking back into the confines of Israel. (This practice gives us the phrase, "Shake the dust off your shoes.") They would not eat food prepared by Gentile hands. They purified utensils purchased from a Gentile before they used them to cook food. Gentiles were considered unclean, and their presence was considered defiling.

We find this attitude in the story of Jonah in the Old Testament. When God called Jonah to carry His message of repentance to the Ninevites, the prophet refused to go because he was afraid the Ninevites would believe the message and turn to God in repentance. Jonah wanted them all to be judged. That is generally the way the Jews felt about the Gentiles.

But God had included the Gentiles in His plan of redemption. He wanted the gospel to go to them . . . and He was going to use Jewish men and women to carry that message. As we have seen, God was in the process of calling Paul to minister to the Gentile world, and He had opened the way for Peter to minister in Lydda and Joppa. But in this next section in Acts, we find one of the turning points in the early church when God speaks directly to Peter about his role in opening the way for the Gentiles to receive the gospel. It all begins while Peter is staying in Joppa at the home a *tanner*—a profession the Jews would have considered unclean.

EXPLORING THE TEXT

Peter's Vision (Acts 10:1–16)

> [1] There was a certain man in Caesarea called Cornelius, a centurion of what was called the Italian Regiment, [2] a devout man and one who feared God with all his household, who gave alms generously to the people, and prayed to God always. [3] About the ninth hour of the day he saw clearly in a vision an angel of God coming in and saying to him, "Cornelius!"
>
> [4] And when he observed him, he was afraid, and said, "What is it, lord?"

So he said to him, "Your prayers and your alms have come up for a memorial before God. [5] Now send men to Joppa, and send for Simon whose surname is Peter. [6] He is lodging with Simon, a tanner, whose house is by the sea. He will tell you what you must do." [7] And when the angel who spoke to him had departed, Cornelius called two of his household servants and a devout soldier from among those who waited on him continually. [8] So when he had explained all these things to them, he sent them to Joppa.

[9] The next day, as they went on their journey and drew near the city, Peter went up on the housetop to pray, about the sixth hour. [10] Then he became very hungry and wanted to eat; but while they made ready, he fell into a trance [11] and saw heaven opened and an object like a great sheet bound at the four corners, descending to him and let down to the earth. [12] In it were all kinds of four-footed animals of the earth, wild beasts, creeping things, and birds of the air. [13] And a voice came to him, "Rise, Peter; kill and eat."

[14] But Peter said, "Not so, Lord! For I have never eaten anything common or unclean."

[15] And a voice spoke to him again the second time, "What God has cleansed you must not call common." [16] This was done three times. And the object was taken up into heaven again.

---

1. Luke tells us that Cornelius was a centurion in the Roman army . . . and thus a Gentile. What was unique about Cornelius? What did the angel say to him (see verses 2–6)?

_____

_____

_____

_____

_____

_____

2. What instructions did Peter receive in his vision? How did the voice respond when Peter refused to associate himself with anything unclean (see verses 13–15)?

_____

_____

_____

_____

_____

Peter Is Summoned to Caesarea (Acts 10:17–33)

¹⁷ Now while Peter wondered within himself what this vision which he had seen meant, behold, the men who had been sent from Cornelius had made inquiry for Simon's house, and stood before the gate. ¹⁸ And they called and asked whether Simon, whose surname was Peter, was lodging there.

¹⁹ While Peter thought about the vision, the Spirit said to him, "Behold, three men are seeking you. ²⁰ Arise therefore, go down and go with them, doubting nothing; for I have sent them."

²¹ Then Peter went down to the men who had been sent to him from Cornelius, and said, "Yes, I am he whom you seek. For what reason have you come?"

²² And they said, "Cornelius the centurion, a just man, one who fears God and has a good reputation among all the nation of the Jews, was divinely instructed by a holy angel to summon you to his house, and to hear words from you." ²³ Then he invited them in and lodged them.

On the next day Peter went away with them, and some brethren from Joppa accompanied him.

²⁴ And the following day they entered Caesarea. Now Cornelius was waiting for them, and had called together his relatives and close friends. ²⁵ As Peter was coming in, Cornelius met him and fell down at his feet and worshiped him. ²⁶ But Peter lifted him up, saying, "Stand up; I myself am also a man." ²⁷ And as he talked with him, he went in

and found many who had come together. ²⁸ Then he said to them, "You know how unlawful it is for a Jewish man to keep company with or go to one of another nation. But God has shown me that I should not call any man common or unclean. ²⁹ Therefore I came without objection as soon as I was sent for. I ask, then, for what reason have you sent for me?"

³⁰ So Cornelius said, "Four days ago I was fasting until this hour; and at the ninth hour I prayed in my house, and behold, a man stood before me in bright clothing, ³¹ and said, 'Cornelius, your prayer has been heard, and your alms are remembered in the sight of God. ³² Send therefore to Joppa and call Simon here, whose surname is Peter. He is lodging in the house of Simon, a tanner, by the sea. When he comes, he will speak to you.' ³³ So I sent to you immediately, and you have done well to come. Now therefore, we are all present before God, to hear all the things commanded you by God."

---

3. How did Peter make the connection between his vision and the visit from Cornelius's delegates (see verses 19–20, 28–29)?

_____

_____

_____

_____

4. Luke tells us that Cornelius fell down at Peter's feet and "worshiped him," which indicates that Cornelius believed Peter held some form of supernatural power. How did Peter correct his misunderstanding? What "laws" did Peter say he was breaking (see verses 25–28)?

_____

_____

_____

_____

Peter in Cornelius's Household (Acts 10:34–48)

[34] Then Peter opened his mouth and said: "In truth I perceive that God shows no partiality. [35] But in every nation whoever fears Him and works righteousness is accepted by Him. [36] The word which God sent to the children of Israel, preaching peace through Jesus Christ—He is Lord of all—[37] that word you know, which was proclaimed throughout all Judea, and began from Galilee after the baptism which John preached: [38] how God anointed Jesus of Nazareth with the Holy Spirit and with power, who went about doing good and healing all who were oppressed by the devil, for God was with Him. [39] And we are witnesses of all things which He did both in the land of the Jews and in Jerusalem, whom they killed by hanging on a tree. [40] Him God raised up on the third day, and showed Him openly, [41] not to all the people, but to witnesses chosen before by God, even to us who ate and drank with Him after He arose from the dead. [42] And He commanded us to preach to the people, and to testify that it is He who was ordained by God to be Judge of the living and the dead. [43] To Him all the prophets witness that, through His name, whoever believes in Him will receive remission of sins."

[44] While Peter was still speaking these words, the Holy Spirit fell upon all those who heard the word. [45] And those of the circumcision who believed were astonished, as many as came with Peter, because the gift of the Holy Spirit had been poured out on the Gentiles also. [46] For they heard them speak with tongues and magnify God.

Then Peter answered, [47] "Can anyone forbid water, that these should not be baptized who have received the Holy Spirit just as we have?" [48] And he commanded them to be baptized in the name of the Lord. Then they asked him to stay a few days.

5. What was at the heart of the message that Peter delivered to the people in Cornelius's household (see verses 39–43)?

_____

_____

_____

_____

_____

6. What happened as Peter was speaking these words? Why were "those of the circumcision"—the Jewish believers who came with Peter—astonished (see verses 45–46)?

_____

_____

_____

_____

_____

_____

Peter Defends God's Grace (Acts 11:1–18)

¹ Now the apostles and brethren who were in Judea heard that the Gentiles had also received the word of God. ² And when Peter came up to Jerusalem, those of the circumcision contended with him, ³ saying, "You went in to uncircumcised men and ate with them!"

⁴ But Peter explained it to them in order from the beginning, saying: ⁵ "I was in the city of Joppa praying; and in a trance I saw a vision, an object descending like a great sheet, let down from heaven by four corners; and it came to me. ⁶ When I observed it intently and considered, I saw four-footed animals of the earth, wild beasts, creeping things, and birds of the air. ⁷ And I heard a voice saying to

me, 'Rise, Peter; kill and eat.' ⁸ But I said, 'Not so, Lord! For nothing common or unclean has at any time entered my mouth.' ⁹ But the voice answered me again from heaven, 'What God has cleansed you must not call common.' ¹⁰ Now this was done three times, and all were drawn up again into heaven. ¹¹ At that very moment, three men stood before the house where I was, having been sent to me from Caesarea. ¹² Then the Spirit told me to go with them, doubting nothing. Moreover these six brethren accompanied me, and we entered the man's house. ¹³ And he told us how he had seen an angel standing in his house, who said to him, 'Send men to Joppa, and call for Simon whose surname is Peter, ¹⁴ who will tell you words by which you and all your household will be saved.' ¹⁵ And as I began to speak, the Holy Spirit fell upon them, as upon us at the beginning. ¹⁶ Then I remembered the word of the Lord, how He said, 'John indeed baptized with water, but you shall be baptized with the Holy Spirit.' ¹⁷ If therefore God gave them the same gift as He gave us when we believed on the Lord Jesus Christ, who was I that I could withstand God?"

¹⁸ When they heard these things they became silent; and they glorified God, saying, "Then God has also granted to the Gentiles repentance to life."

---

7. What accusation did the Jewish believers make against Peter when he returned to Jerusalem (see verse 3)?

_____

_____

_____

_____

_____

_____

8. What did Peter say that led these believers to understand God had accepted the Gentiles and offered them entrance into His kingdom (see verses 15–17)?

_____

_____

_____

_____

_____

_____

REVIEWING THE STORY

One of the most important events in the history of Christianity began with a pair of visions. A Roman centurion named Cornelius had a vision of an angel, who told him to send for the apostle Peter. Meanwhile, Peter had a vision in which God told him to eat animals that the Jewish people considered unclean. When representatives from Cornelius then arrived in Joppa, the apostle realized that he was being called to spread the gospel to the Gentiles. Later, Peter defended his actions to the Jewish believers in Jerusalem, explaining the Holy Spirit had fallen on the Gentiles just as He had fallen on them on the Day of Pentecost. The Jewish believers then glorified God for also granting the Gentiles repentance and salvation.

9. How did God challenge Peter's traditional Jewish beliefs about what the Lord considered clean and unclean (see Acts 10:12–15)?

_____

_____

_____

_____

_____

10. What did Peter say to Cornelius when he had entered his home (see Acts 10:28–29)?

_____

_____

_____

_____

_____

11. What did Peter mean when he said that God shows no partiality (see Acts 10:34–35)?

_____

_____

_____

_____

12. How did Peter's accusers react when he told them the whole story of his encounter with Cornelius (see Acts 11:18)?

_____

_____

_____

_____

APPLYING THE MESSAGE

13. What are some reasons why divisions still exist within the church?

_____

_____

_____

_____

_____

14. What boundaries has God called you to cross in order to share the gospel with others?

_____

_____

_____

_____

_____

REFLECTING ON THE MEANING

"In truth I perceive that God shows no partiality" (Acts 10:34). That verse is Peter's summation of what God had taught him through his vision. God had to drop a sheet down from heaven in his lap . . . but Peter got the message. His experience in this section of Acts actually shines a light on our own prejudices. It teaches us we are not to call _unclean_ what God has _cleansed_. If God has cleansed people, they are a part of who we are. They may not sing like we do, teach like we do, or worship like we do, but we are not to cast them in any kind of disparaging categories.

It is surprising just how many times the Bible warns us about this type of offense. In the Old Testament, the Lord warned the people to "do no injustice in judgment" (Leviticus 19:15) and to not "show partiality in judgment [but] hear the small as well as the great" (Deuteronomy 1:17). In the New Testament, the apostle Paul echoes Peter's words that "there is no partiality with God" (Romans 2:11), and "he who does wrong will be repaid for what he has done . . . there is no partiality" (Colossians 3:25). Peter himself would later write that "the Father . . . without partiality judges according to each one's work" (1 Peter 1:17).

Just consider the cross. The vertical beam is longer than the horizontal beam, which is symbolic of the vertical beam reaching high and upward to God—while the horizontal beam is symbolically reaching outward to the level of all humankind. In the cross, we reach high, but we stay on the level to minister to all humankind. When we come to believe in the Christ of

71

this cross, our concern, our love, and our service must be willing to reach outward to humankind as we level with one another, without the thought of status in life or of race.

JOURNALING YOUR RESPONSE

What are some ways that you have shown partiality to certain people in the past? What can you do today to treat all people the way God treats them?

THE POWER OF PRAYER

Acts 12:1–14:28

GETTING STARTED

What are some remarkable things you have seen happen because of prayer?

_____

_____

_____

_____

_____

_____

_____

_____

_____

_____

_____

_____

_____

_____

SETTING THE STAGE

There have been many famous prayer meetings throughout the history of the church. For instance, on August 13, 1727, a community located in Herrnhut, Germany, commenced a round-the-clock prayer watch that sparked the Moravian Revival, which lasted for more than 100 years. During the first twenty-five years of that revival, the Lord called more than 100 missionaries to serve around the world.

In August 1806, five college students from Massachusetts gathered in a field to discuss the state of missions in Asia. When their meeting was interrupted by a thunderstorm, they sought shelter inside a haystack and prayed until the skies cleared. The "Haystack Prayer Meeting," as it came to be called, began a stream of witness that flowed out of America and into all parts of the world. Many scholars believe it is the key event that developed American Protestant missions for decades to follow.

On September 23, 1857, a minister named Jeremy Lanphier started a prayer meeting in the lecture room of the old Dutch Reformed Church on Fulton Street in New York City. Only six people responded to his advertisement on that day. But when the stock market crashed on October 10 of that year, people began to flock to the meetings. Within six months, nearly 10,000 people were gathering daily for prayer in New York City alone. Out of that prayer meeting grew a widespread revival that lasted for years.

God uses great prayer meetings to accomplish significant things. Every revival that has ever happened started with a prayer meeting. Yet few can rival the importance of the one that took place in Antioch around AD 46, shortly after the death of the disciple James at the hands of King Herod Agrippa. This meeting represents a watershed moment in the history of the church, for it was there the Holy Spirit officially commissioned Paul and Barnabas to spread the gospel.

EXPLORING THE TEXT

Herod's Violence to the Church (Acts 12:1–19)

> [1] Now about that time Herod the king stretched out his hand to harass some from the church. [2] Then he killed James the brother of John with the sword. [3] And because he saw that it pleased the Jews,

he proceeded further to seize Peter also. Now it was during the Days of Unleavened Bread. ⁴ So when he had arrested him, he put him in prison, and delivered him to four squads of soldiers to keep him, intending to bring him before the people after Passover.

⁵ Peter was therefore kept in prison, but constant prayer was offered to God for him by the church. ⁶ And when Herod was about to bring him out, that night Peter was sleeping, bound with two chains between two soldiers; and the guards before the door were keeping the prison. ⁷ Now behold, an angel of the Lord stood by him, and a light shone in the prison; and he struck Peter on the side and raised him up, saying, "Arise quickly!" And his chains fell off his hands. ⁸ Then the angel said to him, "Gird yourself and tie on your sandals"; and so he did. And he said to him, "Put on your garment and follow me." ⁹ So he went out and followed him, and did not know that what was done by the angel was real, but thought he was seeing a vision. ¹⁰ When they were past the first and the second guard posts, they came to the iron gate that leads to the city, which opened to them of its own accord; and they went out and went down one street, and immediately the angel departed from him.

¹¹ And when Peter had come to himself, he said, "Now I know for certain that the Lord has sent His angel, and has delivered me from the hand of Herod and from all the expectation of the Jewish people."

---

1. King Herod Agrippa viewed the Christians as a divisive and disruptive element in the region of Judea. Given this, after killing James, why did he continue his persecution by arresting Peter? What was his plan for Peter's trial (see verses 3–4)?

_____

_____

_____

_____

2. What did the believers do when they learned Peter had been imprisoned? How did Peter react when the angel appeared in the prison (see verses 5–9)?

_____

_____

_____

_____

_____

Barnabas and Saul Are Sent Out (Acts 13:1–12)

¹ Now in the church that was at Antioch there were certain prophets and teachers: Barnabas, Simeon who was called Niger, Lucius of Cyrene, Manaen who had been brought up with Herod the tetrarch, and Saul. ² As they ministered to the Lord and fasted, the Holy Spirit said, "Now separate to Me Barnabas and Saul for the work to which I have called them." ³ Then, having fasted and prayed, and laid hands on them, they sent them away.

⁴ So, being sent out by the Holy Spirit, they went down to Seleucia, and from there they sailed to Cyprus. ⁵ And when they arrived in Salamis, they preached the word of God in the synagogues of the Jews. They also had John as their assistant.

⁶ Now when they had gone through the island to Paphos, they found a certain sorcerer, a false prophet, a Jew whose name was Bar-Jesus, ⁷ who was with the proconsul, Sergius Paulus, an intelligent man. This man called for Barnabas and Saul and sought to hear the word of God. ⁸ But Elymas the sorcerer (for so his name is translated) withstood them, seeking to turn the proconsul away from the faith. ⁹ Then Saul, who also is called Paul, filled with the Holy Spirit, looked intently at him ¹⁰ and said, "O full of all deceit and all fraud, you son of the devil, you enemy of all righteousness, will you not cease perverting the straight ways of the Lord? ¹¹ And now, indeed, the

hand of the Lord is upon you, and you shall be blind, not seeing the sun for a time."

And immediately a dark mist fell on him, and he went around seeking someone to lead him by the hand. [12] Then the proconsul believed, when he saw what had been done, being astonished at the teaching of the Lord.

---

3. What events transpired that led to the elders in Antioch sending out Barnabas and Paul as missionaries? Where did Paul and Barnabas go first (see verses 1–5)?

_____

_____

_____

_____

4. Sergius Paulus, the Roman proconsul of Paphos, made an official inquiry into the work Paul and Barnabas in order to hear the word of God. How did Bar-Jesus, a false prophet, react to this inquiry? What happened to him as a result (see verses 8–11)?

_____

_____

_____

_____

Paul and Barnabas in Antioch of Pisidia (Acts 13:42–46)

[42] So when the Jews went out of the synagogue, the Gentiles begged that these words might be preached to them the next Sabbath. [43] Now when the congregation had broken up, many of the Jews

and devout proselytes followed Paul and Barnabas, who, speaking to them, persuaded them to continue in the grace of God.

⁴⁴ On the next Sabbath almost the whole city came together to hear the word of God. ⁴⁵ But when the Jews saw the multitudes, they were filled with envy; and contradicting and blaspheming, they opposed the things spoken by Paul. ⁴⁶ Then Paul and Barnabas grew bold and said, "It was necessary that the word of God should be spoken to you first; but since you reject it, and judge yourselves unworthy of everlasting life, behold, we turn to the Gentiles."

⁴⁷ For this is what the Lord has commanded us:

"'I have made you a light for the Gentiles,

that you may bring salvation to the ends of the earth.'"

⁴⁸ When the Gentiles heard this, they were glad and honored the word of the Lord; and all who were appointed for eternal life believed.

⁴⁹ The word of the Lord spread through the whole region. ⁵⁰ But the Jewish leaders incited the God-fearing women of high standing and the leading men of the city. They stirred up persecution against Paul and Barnabas, and expelled them from their region. ⁵¹ So they shook the dust off their feet as a warning to them and went to Iconium. ⁵² And the disciples were filled with joy and with the Holy Spirit.

5. Paul and Barnabas's journey continued to Antioch in Pisidia, located in modern-day Turkey. It was here that Paul established his typical pattern for ministry, beginning by teaching in the synagogue, and then moving to direct ministry to the Gentiles. How did the Gentiles react to Paul's teaching? How did the Jews in the city react (see verses 42–45)?

6. How did the Jewish leaders of Antioch react when they saw that almost the entire city had gathered to hear Paul speak (see verse 45)?

_____

_____

_____

_____

_____

_____

_____

Idolatry at Lystra (Acts 14:8–20)

[8] And in Lystra a certain man without strength in his feet was sitting, a cripple from his mother's womb, who had never walked. [9] This man heard Paul speaking. Paul, observing him intently and seeing that he had faith to be healed, [10] said with a loud voice, "Stand up straight on your feet!" And he leaped and walked. [11] Now when the people saw what Paul had done, they raised their voices, saying in the Lycaonian language, "The gods have come down to us in the likeness of men!" [12] And Barnabas they called Zeus, and Paul, Hermes, because he was the chief speaker. [13] Then the priest of Zeus, whose temple was in front of their city, brought oxen and garlands to the gates, intending to sacrifice with the multitudes.

[14] But when the apostles Barnabas and Paul heard this, they tore their clothes and ran in among the multitude, crying out [15] and saying, "Men, why are you doing these things? We also are men with the same nature as you, and preach to you that you should turn from these useless things to the living God, who made the heaven, the earth, the sea, and all things that are in them, [16] who in bygone generations allowed all nations to walk in their own ways. [17] Nevertheless He did not leave Himself without witness, in that He

did good, gave us rain from heaven and fruitful seasons, filling our hearts with food and gladness." [18] And with these sayings they could scarcely restrain the multitudes from sacrificing to them.

[19] Then Jews from Antioch and Iconium came there; and having persuaded the multitudes, they stoned Paul and dragged him out of the city, supposing him to be dead. [20] However, when the disciples gathered around him, he rose up and went into the city. And the next day he departed with Barnabas to Derbe.

---

7. How did the people of Lystra react when they saw that Paul had healed the crippled man (see verses 11–13)?

_____

_____

_____

_____

_____

_____

_____

_____

8. How did Paul and Barnabas respond to the worship they received from the people of Lystra (see verses 14–18)?

_____

_____

_____

_____

_____

_____

REVIEWING THE STORY

Herod intensified his persecution by putting James to death and arresting Peter. The church responded by praying, and God sent an angel to free Peter from his prison cell. Peter made his way to the house of Mary, the mother of John, to let his fellow believers know about his miraculous escape. Meanwhile, in Cyprus, Paul and Barnabas encountered a sorcerer who tried to prevent them from sharing the gospel with a local proconsul. The sorcerer was struck blind. In Antioch, Paul preached the gospel to the Jews in the synagogue. Afterward, the Gentiles in the city asked him to preach to them. In Lystra, Paul healed a crippled man. The people of Lystra began to worship him and Barnabas as gods until they put an end to it.

9. How did the angel of the Lord assist in Peter's escape from prison (see Acts 12:7–10)?

_____

_____

_____

_____

_____

10. How did the Holy Spirit respond to the urgent prayer and fasting at the church in Antioch (see Acts 13:2)?

_____

_____

_____

_____

_____

11. How did Paul explain to the Jewish people at Antioch in Pisidia his reasoning for sharing the gospel with the Gentiles (see Acts 13:46)?

_____

_____

_____

_____

_____

_____

12. What happened when the Jews from Antioch in Pisidia and Iconium arrived in the town of Lystra where Paul and Barnabas were ministering (see Acts 14:19)?

_____

_____

_____

_____

_____

_____

_____

APPLYING THE MESSAGE

13. What need—in your life, your family, your church, your community, or the world—calls for your urgent prayer right now?

_____

_____

_____

_____

_____

14. How do you deal with people who try to interfere with your sharing of the gospel?

_____

_____

_____

_____

_____

REFLECTING ON THE MEANING

Peter and the members of the early church faced an impossible challenge when Herod began his persecution. They lost James, one of Jesus' closest disciples and a leader in the community, and they almost lost Peter. Yet in the midst of that challenge, the members of the early church discovered God's power is best displayed in impossible situations.

Sometimes we don't see the power of God in our lives because we are living in a "safe zone." If we never face impossible situations, we never get to see the full power of God. As missionary William Carey said, "Expect great things from God, and attempt great things for God." When we do this, we may find ourselves in impossible situations—but we will also find ourselves in circumstances where we can witness the full glory and deliverance of God. We can see God break through to do what we could never do.

A Christian leader named Carl Bates once prayed, "God, I want Your power." As time wore on, however, he realized that he had not received this power from God. One day, when he was burdened more than he could bear, he asked, "God, why haven't You answered my prayer for Your power?" He seemed to hear God whisper in his ear, "Bates, with plans no bigger than yours, you don't need My power."

If we don't ask God for anything big, we won't see His power. So, be thankful for impossible situations and pray in the midst of them. This section in Acts teaches us that God's power is best displayed in challenging experiences. Our difficulties become God's opportunities. If you are in an impossible situation, you are in a position to say, "God, do something so marvelous that You're the only One who can ever take credit for it."

JOURNALING YOUR RESPONSE

What is the closest thing to an impossible situation in your life right now? How are you relying on God's power during this challenging time?

THE CHURCH IN CONFLICT

Acts 15:1–16:40

GETTING STARTED

What are some conflicts today that often rise up among believers in Christ?

_____

_____

_____

_____

_____

_____

_____

_____

_____

_____

_____

_____

_____

_____

_____

_____

_____

_____

_____

SETTING THE STAGE

Throughout the history of the church, there have been important councils that have met to decide issues related to church doctrine. Most church historians recognize seven great councils, starting way back in the early days of the church. One of the most important of these was the First Council of Nicaea, which was convened in AD 325. This council resulted in the first uniform Christian doctrine, which we know today as the Nicene Creed.

Another important meeting was the Council of Chalcedon, held in AD 451. At this council, the leaders created the Confession of Chalcedon, in which they provided a clear statement (to counter heretical doctrine that was circulating at the time) as to the human and divine nature of Christ. Both councils dealt with the person and work of Jesus Christ—who He was, what His work was all about, His divinity, and His humanity.

However, the work of the council mentioned in this next section of Acts—what scholars call the "Magna Carta" of the church—may be the most significant of all. In this apostolic council based in Jerusalem, the issue at stake concerned the very nature of salvation. The church needed to decide what a person—whether a Jew or a Gentile—was required to do in order to be saved. This debate had sprung up gradually as more and more Gentiles were entering into the church . . . and the council needed to decide if those Gentile believers needed to adopt Jewish practices in order to be saved.

EXPLORING THE TEXT

Conflict in the Church (Acts 15:1–12)

[1] And certain men came down from Judea and taught the brethren, "Unless you are circumcised according to the custom of Moses, you cannot be saved." [2] Therefore, when Paul and Barnabas had no small dissension and dispute with them, they determined that Paul and Barnabas and certain others of them should go up to Jerusalem, to the apostles and elders, about this question.

³ So, being sent on their way by the church, they passed through Phoenicia and Samaria, describing the conversion of the Gentiles; and they caused great joy to all the brethren. ⁴ And when they had come to Jerusalem, they were received by the church and the apostles and the elders; and they reported all things that God had done with them. ⁵ But some of the sect of the Pharisees who believed rose up, saying, "It is necessary to circumcise them, and to command them to keep the law of Moses."

⁶ Now the apostles and elders came together to consider this matter. ⁷ And when there had been much dispute, Peter rose up and said to them: "Men and brethren, you know that a good while ago God chose among us, that by my mouth the Gentiles should hear the word of the gospel and believe. ⁸ So God, who knows the heart, acknowledged them by giving them the Holy Spirit, just as He did to us, ⁹ and made no distinction between us and them, purifying their hearts by faith. ¹⁰ Now therefore, why do you test God by putting a yoke on the neck of the disciples which neither our fathers nor we were able to bear? ¹¹ But we believe that through the grace of the Lord Jesus Christ we shall be saved in the same manner as they."

¹² Then all the multitude kept silent and listened to Barnabas and Paul declaring how many miracles and wonders God had worked through them among the Gentiles.

---

1. How did the men from Judea complicate the lives of the converted Gentiles? How did Paul and Barnabas react to what the Jews were proclaiming (see verses 1–2)?

_____

_____

_____

_____

_____

2. What did the elders of the church do to resolve to controversy? What did Peter say regarding the matter at hand (see verses 6–11)?

_____

_____

_____

_____

_____

_____

Timothy and the Macedonian Call (Acts 16:1–10)

¹ Then [Paul] came to Derbe and Lystra. And behold, a certain disciple was there, named Timothy, the son of a certain Jewish woman who believed, but his father was Greek. ² He was well spoken of by the brethren who were at Lystra and Iconium. ³ Paul wanted to have him go on with him. And he took him and circumcised him because of the Jews who were in that region, for they all knew that his father was Greek. ⁴ And as they went through the cities, they delivered to them the decrees to keep, which were determined by the apostles and elders at Jerusalem. ⁵ So the churches were strengthened in the faith, and increased in number daily.

⁶ Now when they had gone through Phrygia and the region of Galatia, they were forbidden by the Holy Spirit to preach the word in Asia. ⁷ After they had come to Mysia, they tried to go into Bithynia, but the Spirit did not permit them. ⁸ So passing by Mysia, they came down to Troas. ⁹ And a vision appeared to Paul in the night. A man of Macedonia stood and pleaded with him, saying, "Come over to Macedonia and help us." ¹⁰ Now after he had seen the vision, immediately we sought to go to Macedonia, concluding that the Lord had called us to preach the gospel to them.

3. As Paul and Barnabas prepared for their second journey, a dispute arose that caused them to part company. Paul chose another companion named Silas, and the two came to Derbe and Lystra. It was there Paul met Timothy, who would come to be a coworker in his mission to the Gentiles. Given all that Paul had just gone through with the Jerusalem Council, why did he agree to let Timothy be circumcised (see verses 1–3)?

_____

_____

_____

_____

_____

_____

_____

4. Why did Paul go to preach the gospel in Macedonia instead of Asia (see verses 6–9)?

_____

_____

_____

_____

_____

_____

_____

Paul and Silas in Philippi (Acts 16:11–19)

[11] Therefore, sailing from Troas, we ran a straight course to Samothrace, and the next day came to Neapolis, [12] and from there to Philippi, which is the foremost city of that part of Macedonia, a colony. And we were staying in that city for some days. [13] And on the Sabbath day we went out of the city to the riverside, where prayer

was customarily made; and we sat down and spoke to the women who met there. ¹⁴ Now a certain woman named Lydia heard us. She was a seller of purple from the city of Thyatira, who worshiped God. The Lord opened her heart to heed the things spoken by Paul. ¹⁵ And when she and her household were baptized, she begged us, saying, "If you have judged me to be faithful to the Lord, come to my house and stay." So she persuaded us.

¹⁶ Now it happened, as we went to prayer, that a certain slave girl possessed with a spirit of divination met us, who brought her masters much profit by fortune-telling. ¹⁷ This girl followed Paul and us, and cried out, saying, "These men are the servants of the Most High God, who proclaim to us the way of salvation." ¹⁸ And this she did for many days.

But Paul, greatly annoyed, turned and said to the spirit, "I command you in the name of Jesus Christ to come out of her." And he came out that very hour. ¹⁹ But when her masters saw that their hope of profit was gone, they seized Paul and Silas and dragged them into the marketplace to the authorities.

---

5. In this section, Luke begins to refer to Paul and his party by using the pronoun *we*, which indicates he might have joined the group in Troas. How did the group encounter Lydia? How did she become an important figure in the early church (see verses 13–15)?

_____

_____

_____

_____

_____

_____

_____

6. What did the demon-possessed slave girl do that annoyed Paul? How did he respond to the issue (see verses 17–18)?

_____

_____

_____

_____

_____

_____

_____

Paul and Silas Imprisoned (Acts 16:20–34)

[20] And they brought them to the magistrates, and said, "These men, being Jews, exceedingly trouble our city; [21] and they teach customs which are not lawful for us, being Romans, to receive or observe." [22] Then the multitude rose up together against them; and the magistrates tore off their clothes and commanded them to be beaten with rods. [23] And when they had laid many stripes on them, they threw them into prison, commanding the jailer to keep them securely. [24] Having received such a charge, he put them into the inner prison and fastened their feet in the stocks.

[25] But at midnight Paul and Silas were praying and singing hymns to God, and the prisoners were listening to them. [26] Suddenly there was a great earthquake, so that the foundations of the prison were shaken; and immediately all the doors were opened and everyone's chains were loosed. [27] And the keeper of the prison, awaking from sleep and seeing the prison doors open, supposing the prisoners had fled, drew his sword and was about to kill himself. [28] But Paul called with a loud voice, saying, "Do yourself no harm, for we are all here."

[29] Then he called for a light, ran in, and fell down trembling before Paul and Silas. [30] And he brought them out and said, "Sirs, what must I do to be saved?"

³¹ So they said, "Believe on the Lord Jesus Christ, and you will be saved, you and your household." ³² Then they spoke the word of the Lord to him and to all who were in his house. ³³ And he took them the same hour of the night and washed their stripes. And immediately he and all his family were baptized. ³⁴ Now when he had brought them into his house, he set food before them; and he rejoiced, having believed in God with all his household.

7. What did Paul and Silas do once they had been thrown in jail? How were they released (see verses 25–26)?

_____

_____

_____

_____

_____

_____

_____

8. How did Paul keep the jailer from killing himself? What did they say the jailer needed to do to receive salvation from Christ (see verses 28–32)?

_____

_____

_____

_____

_____

_____

_____

REVIEWING THE STORY

The issue of whether the Gentiles coming into the church had to follow Jewish practices to be considered Christians finally came to a boiling point. Paul appealed to the leaders of the Jerusalem church to rule on the matter, and the council ultimately issued a decree that said the new believers did *not* have to obey Jewish law. Paul had a disagreement with Barnabas, resulting in the two parting ways. Paul instead chose Silas as a companion for his second missionary journey, and they came to Lystra (where they met Timothy) and Troas (where they likely met Luke). It was there the Holy Spirit directed Paul and his companions to Macedonia, and the group crossed into Europe. In the city of Philippi, Paul and Silas met a woman named Lydia and were jailed for healing a demon-possessed girl. An earthquake freed them, but Paul and his fellow prisoners did not leave. The grateful jailer asked how he could be saved.

9. What was the main issue on which the Jerusalem Council needed to rule (see Acts 15:1, 5)?

_____

_____

_____

_____

10. What was the result of Paul, Silas, and Timothy's missionary work in Derbe, Lystra, and other cities in the region (see Acts 16:5)?

_____

_____

_____

_____

_____

11. In the city of Philippi, why did the masters of the slave girl seize Paul and Silas after they drove the demon from her (see Acts 16:19)?

_____

_____

_____

_____

_____

_____

12. What kind of suffering did Paul and Silas endure in prison (see Acts 16:20–24)?

_____

_____

_____

_____

_____

APPLYING THE MESSAGE

13. Where do you think the Holy Spirit is guiding you to serve?

_____

_____

_____

_____

_____

14. What would you say to a friend who asked what he or she needed to do to be saved?

_____

_____

_____

_____

_____

REFLECTING ON THE MEANING

One of the keys to meaningful Christian ministry is having the right purpose. In this section in Acts, we find that Paul had three such purposes. The first was *edification*. Paul's second missionary journey sprang from his desire to revisit the churches that he and Barnabas had founded on their first journey. His connection with converts did not end at baptism. He was committed to discipleship and cared deeply about the welfare of these new converts.

Paul's concern for shepherding the new believers is a great example to us. Luke uses the word *strengthened* in Acts 16:5 to describe Paul's work in the churches he planted. He built new believers up and strengthened them in their walk with Christ. No matter who we are or what God has called us to do, we are needed in the church to build up one another in the faith.

The second purpose that Paul had was *encouragement*. The new converts had been under pressure from Jewish believers who insisted they obey the Jewish law. The church leaders in Jerusalem wrote a letter to these new converts, informing them that they *didn't* have to follow the demands of the law. Paul and Barnabas brought the letter with them to encourage the new believers and assure them that the Almighty God, through His Son, Jesus Christ, had given them freedom to live the life that they wanted to live in Jesus Christ.

The third purpose that Paul had was *evangelism*. Luke informs us that the churches "increased in number daily" (Acts 16:5). Someone once said that either we evangelize . . . or we fossilize. In church terms, if we don't evangelize, we begin to die.

JOURNALING YOUR RESPONSE

How is God calling you to edify, encourage, and evangelize this week?

A COURAGEOUS LIFE

Acts 17:1–20:38

GETTING STARTED

What criticism have you faced because of your Christian faith? How have you responded?

_____

_____

_____

_____

_____

_____

_____

_____

_____

_____

_____

SETTING THE STAGE

As you study the book of Acts, you have to wonder at the courage of Paul. It seems as if he encountered trials, troubles, and tribulations everywhere he went. He often received criticism when he preached the message of the gospel in a new place. When he wasn't struggling with the authorities in the region and the attitudes of the locals, there was typically a Jewish community nearby who opposed his message and tried run him out of town. It seemed everything he did either caused a revival or a riot—sometimes both.

This is the scene as we begin this next section of Acts. Paul is on his second missionary journey, accompanied by Silas and Timothy, and they have been asked to leave the city of Philippi in the wake of a riot provoked by Paul's healing of a demon-possessed girl. Paul and Silas had been attacked by the crowds, beaten with rods by the authorities, and then thrown into prison for the night. These events—and undoubtedly the pain of the beatings they endured—were still vivid in their memories as they traveled to the next stop. This time, they are making a three-day trek to the city of Thessalonica, which was located thirty-three miles southeast of Philippi.

In spite of the setbacks, Luke never states their pace ever slowed or the pain overshadowed their zeal for spreading the gospel of Christ. There is no hint of dread on the part of Paul and his companions about the likelihood of further rejection and persecution (which *will* happen in this city). Rather, they eagerly anticipate the opportunities that await them in a new place. Paul and Silas have been beaten, but they have not given up. Their bodies are battered, but their resolve to carry out the will of God is as healthy as ever.

EXPLORING THE TEXT

Paul in Thessalonica and Berea (Acts 17:1–13)

---

¹ Now when they had passed through Amphipolis and Apollonia, they came to Thessalonica, where there was a synagogue of the Jews. ² Then Paul, as his custom was, went in to them, and for three Sabbaths reasoned with them from the Scriptures, ³ explaining and demonstrating that the Christ had to suffer and rise again from the dead, and saying, "This Jesus whom I preach to you is the Christ." ⁴ And some of them were persuaded; and a great multitude of the devout Greeks, and not a few of the leading women, joined Paul and Silas.

⁵ But the Jews who were not persuaded, becoming envious, took some of the evil men from the marketplace, and gathering a mob,

set all the city in an uproar and attacked the house of Jason, and sought to bring them out to the people. ⁶ But when they did not find them, they dragged Jason and some brethren to the rulers of the city, crying out, "These who have turned the world upside down have come here too. ⁷ Jason has harbored them, and these are all acting contrary to the decrees of Caesar, saying there is another king—Jesus." ⁸ And they troubled the crowd and the rulers of the city when they heard these things. ⁹ So when they had taken security from Jason and the rest, they let them go.

¹⁰ Then the brethren immediately sent Paul and Silas away by night to Berea. When they arrived, they went into the synagogue of the Jews. ¹¹ These were more fair-minded than those in Thessalonica, in that they received the word with all readiness, and searched the Scriptures daily to find out whether these things were so. ¹² Therefore many of them believed, and also not a few of the Greeks, prominent women as well as men. ¹³ But when the Jews from Thessalonica learned that the word of God was preached by Paul at Berea, they came there also and stirred up the crowds. ¹⁴ Then immediately the brethren sent Paul away, to go to the sea; but both Silas and Timothy remained there. ¹⁵ So those who conducted Paul brought him to Athens; and receiving a command for Silas and Timothy to come to him with all speed, they departed.

---

1. When Paul arrived in Thessalonica, he followed his typical pattern of first preaching in the local Jewish synagogue. What response did he receive this time (see verses 2–5)?

_____

_____

_____

_____

_____

_____

2. How did Paul and Silas's reception in Berea differ from their experience in Thessalonica? What ultimately caused trouble for them in Berea (see verses 10–13)?

_____

_____

_____

_____

_____

The Philosophers at Athens (Acts 17:16–31)

16 Now while Paul waited for them at Athens, his spirit was provoked within him when he saw that the city was given over to idols. 17 Therefore he reasoned in the synagogue with the Jews and with the Gentile worshipers, and in the marketplace daily with those who happened to be there. 18 Then certain Epicurean and Stoic philosophers encountered him. And some said, "What does this babbler want to say?"

Others said, "He seems to be a proclaimer of foreign gods," because he preached to them Jesus and the resurrection.

19 And they took him and brought him to the Areopagus, saying, "May we know what this new doctrine is of which you speak? 20 For you are bringing some strange things to our ears. Therefore we want to know what these things mean." 21 For all the Athenians and the foreigners who were there spent their time in nothing else but either to tell or to hear some new thing.

22 Then Paul stood in the midst of the Areopagus and said, "Men of Athens, I perceive that in all things you are very religious; 23 for as I was passing through and considering the objects of your worship, I even found an altar with this inscription:

TO THE UNKNOWN GOD.

Therefore, the One whom you worship without knowing, Him I proclaim to you: ²⁴ God, who made the world and everything in it, since He is Lord of heaven and earth, does not dwell in temples made with hands. ²⁵ Nor is He worshiped with men's hands, as though He needed anything, since He gives to all life, breath, and all things. ²⁶ And He has made from one blood every nation of men to dwell on all the face of the earth, and has determined their preappointed times and the boundaries of their dwellings, ²⁷ so that they should seek the Lord, in the hope that they might grope for Him and find Him, though He is not far from each one of us; ²⁸ for in Him we live and move and have our being, as also some of your own poets have said, 'For we are also His offspring.' ²⁹ Therefore, since we are the offspring of God, we ought not to think that the Divine Nature is like gold or silver or stone, something shaped by art and man's devising. ³⁰ Truly, these times of ignorance God overlooked, but now commands all men everywhere to repent, ³¹ because He has appointed a day on which He will judge the world in righteousness by the Man whom He has ordained. He has given assurance of this to all by raising Him from the dead."

---

3. Paul's next stop was in Athens to wait for the arrival of Silas and Timothy. While it seems he had originally not intended to preach there, it appears the rampant idolatry he saw compelled him to present the message of Christ to the Jews and God-fearing Gentiles of the city. How does Luke describe the attitude of the people (see verses 18–21)?

4. What tactic did Paul employ to deliver the gospel to the Athenians? What call to action did he stress the people needed to make (see verses 22–25, 30–31)?

_____

_____

_____

_____

_____

Ministering at Corinth (Acts 18:1–17)

¹ After these things Paul departed from Athens and went to Corinth. ² And he found a certain Jew named Aquila, born in Pontus, who had recently come from Italy with his wife Priscilla (because Claudius had commanded all the Jews to depart from Rome); and he came to them. ³ So, because he was of the same trade, he stayed with them and worked; for by occupation they were tentmakers. ⁴ And he reasoned in the synagogue every Sabbath, and persuaded both Jews and Greeks.

⁵ When Silas and Timothy had come from Macedonia, Paul was compelled by the Spirit, and testified to the Jews that Jesus is the Christ. ⁶ But when they opposed him and blasphemed, he shook his garments and said to them, "Your blood be upon your own heads; I am clean. From now on I will go to the Gentiles." ⁷ And he departed from there and entered the house of a certain man named Justus, one who worshiped God, whose house was next door to the synagogue. ⁸ Then Crispus, the ruler of the synagogue, believed on the Lord with all his household. And many of the Corinthians, hearing, believed and were baptized.

⁹ Now the Lord spoke to Paul in the night by a vision, "Do not be afraid, but speak, and do not keep silent; ¹⁰ for I am with you, and no one will attack you to hurt you; for I have many people in this city." ¹¹ And he continued there a year and six months, teaching the word of God among them.

¹² When Gallio was proconsul of Achaia, the Jews with one accord rose up against Paul and brought him to the judgment seat, ¹³ saying, "This fellow persuades men to worship God contrary to the law."

¹⁴ And when Paul was about to open his mouth, Gallio said to the Jews, "If it were a matter of wrongdoing or wicked crimes, O Jews, there would be reason why I should bear with you. ¹⁵ But if it is a question of words and names and your own law, look to it yourselves; for I do not want to be a judge of such matters." ¹⁶ And he drove them from the judgment seat. ¹⁷ Then all the Greeks took Sosthenes, the ruler of the synagogue, and beat him before the judgment seat. But Gallio took no notice of these things.

---

5. Paul came to Corinth "in weakness, in fear, and in much trembling" (1 Corinthians 2:3). The Holy Spirit had directed him to minister in Macedonia, but so far that mission had not gone well. How did his situation seem to change when he arrived in Corinth? What did he have in common with Priscilla and Aquila, his new allies in the faith (see Acts 18:2–4)?

_____

_____

_____

_____

6. Paul stayed in Corinth for a year and a half, seemingly without any incident. What ultimately compelled Paul and his companions to move on (see verses 12–17)?

_____

_____

_____

_____

Miracles Glorify Christ (Acts 19:11–20)

[11] Now God worked unusual miracles by the hands of Paul, [12] so that even handkerchiefs or aprons were brought from his body to the sick, and the diseases left them and the evil spirits went out of them. [13] Then some of the itinerant Jewish exorcists took it upon themselves to call the name of the Lord Jesus over those who had evil spirits, saying, "We exorcise you by the Jesus whom Paul preaches." [14] Also there were seven sons of Sceva, a Jewish chief priest, who did so.

[15] And the evil spirit answered and said, "Jesus I know, and Paul I know; but who are you?"

[16] Then the man in whom the evil spirit was leaped on them, overpowered them, and prevailed against them, so that they fled out of that house naked and wounded. [17] This became known both to all Jews and Greeks dwelling in Ephesus; and fear fell on them all, and the name of the Lord Jesus was magnified. [18] And many who had believed came confessing and telling their deeds. [19] Also, many of those who had practiced magic brought their books together and burned them in the sight of all. And they counted up the value of them, and it totaled fifty thousand pieces of silver. [20] So the word of the Lord grew mightily and prevailed.

---

7. Paul left Corinth and eventually returned to Antioch. He stayed there for some time, and then departed on his third missionary journey, first stopping in Ephesus. What miracles happened there? Why couldn't the Jewish exorcists do the same (see verses 11–15)?

_____

_____

_____

_____

_____

8. How did the people of Ephesus respond to this event? How did this serve to foster a sort of "revival" in the city (see verses 17–19)?

_____

_____

_____

_____

_____

_____

REVIEWING THE STORY

Paul enraged certain Jews in Thessalonica by sharing the gospel with Gentiles. Paul's enemies formed a vigilante mob and led an assault on the people who had been harboring them. Paul moved on to Berea, where his message was better received. But when the mob from Thessalonica followed him to Berea, Paul left for Athens, where he preached about God's supremacy in the midst of rampant idolatry. From there Paul moved on to Corinth, where he remained for some time before another Jewish mob stirred up trouble, and finally returned to Antioch. He soon embarked for his third missionary journey, staying a while in the city of Ephesus. God performed many miracles there through him, while others—who tried to claim the same power—found out the hard way they could not exorcise demons.

9. What was noteworthy about the people who were persuaded to become Christians in Thessalonica (see Acts 17:4)?

_____

_____

_____

_____

_____

_____

10. Why did Paul rouse the interest of audiences in the city of Athens (see Acts 17:21)?

_____

_____

_____

_____

11. What words of encouragement did God offer to Paul in the city of Corinth as he endured what seemed to be one setback after another (see Acts 18:9–10)?

_____

_____

_____

_____

12. What happened to the Jewish exorcists in the city of Ephesus who tried to drive out a demon "by the Jesus whom Paul preaches" (see Acts 19:17–20)?

_____

_____

_____

_____

APPLYING THE MESSAGE

13. What is the best strategy for dealing with the oppression or suffering that results from your Christian faith?

_____

_____

_____

_____

_____

14. How can you recognize false teachers who, like the Jewish exorcists, try to claim power and authority they don't really have?

_____

_____

_____

_____

_____

REFLECTING ON THE MEANING

While Paul was staying in the city of Corinth, he received an important message from God that said, in effect, "Don't be afraid. Don't be silent. Don't quit now. For I am with you."

Have you ever noticed how many times in the Bible that message comes through to God's people? When Jacob camped by the River Jabbok in fear of his brother, Esau, the Lord met him there and blessed him. When the Israelites were preparing to enter the Promised Land, the Lord told them, "Be strong and of good courage . . . for the LORD your God, He is the One who goes with you" (Deuteronomy 31:6).

God said the same to Joshua when he assumed the leadership of the people: "The LORD your God is with you wherever you go (Joshua 1:9).

Whenever we get discouraged, we need to remember that God hasn't forgotten us. Whenever we are going through a difficult time and it seems as if we're all alone, we need to remember that God has promised, "I will never leave you nor forsake you" (Hebrews 13:5). This knowledge sustained Paul throughout his ministry and gave him the courage to keep going. Paul faced one crisis after another and paid a heavy price for his commitment to the gospel. Yet in every crisis and challenge, he knew that God was with him. At the end of his life, he could look back and say, "The Lord stood with me and strengthened me, so that the message might be preached fully through me, and that all the Gentiles might hear" (2 Timothy 4:17).

When you are facing challenges, nothing will sustain you more than realizing the Almighty God of the universe is with you. He will give you the courage to move forward—if you choose to trust in Him. As Paul wrote, "If God is for us, who can be against us?" (Romans 8:31).

JOURNALING YOUR RESPONSE

What situation are you facing right now in which you need to be reminded God is with you?

_____

_____

_____

_____

_____

_____

_____

_____

_____

_____

_____

_____

_____

_____

_____

_____

_____

_____

_____

_____

_____

PERSEVERING FOR CHRIST

Acts 21:1–23:35

GETTING STARTED

What is the riskiest thing you have ever done in service to the Lord?

_____

_____

_____

_____

_____

_____

_____

_____

_____

_____

_____

SETTING THE STAGE

The Bible is filled with examples of men and women who were courageous in carrying out the will of God. Against all odds—and against the advice of their own friends—they stood for God even if it meant standing against all others. Noah continued building the ark when the people of his day criticized him. For 120 years, he withstood their taunts as he did what

God called him to do. Joshua and Caleb stood apart from their ten fellow spies, who came back from Canaan and said, "The land is filled with giants. We can't go there." They alone saw the potential for God's victory. David stood alone against the giant Goliath. He believed God was all he needed to defeat his enemy. The soldiers cowered, but David said, "The Lord is able to deliver us."

Throughout the history of God's people, men and women of faith have dared to follow Him, even when to do so meant suffering . . . and sometimes death. The apostle Paul was no exception. In his first and second missionary journeys, he faced all kinds of hardships and opposition from the people he was trying to reach with the gospel. The same became true of his third missionary journey. A riot by the local craftsmen forced Paul to flee Ephesus. Jews plotted against him when he reached Greece. In Miletus, he sent for the elders of the Ephesian church, knowing that his return to Jerusalem to carry relief funds from the Gentile churches to the suffering believers in that city would bring him prison and hardships.

Yet Paul is determined to press on in spite of the struggles of the past and the trials he knows are to come. He tells the Ephesian elders, "Now I go bound in the spirit to Jerusalem, not knowing the things that will happen to me there, except that the Holy Spirit testifies in every city, saying that chains and tribulations await me" (Acts 20:22–23). Paul knows that God has a mission and a purpose for him. So he chooses to press on until the end.

EXPLORING THE TEXT

Warnings on the Journey to Jerusalem (Acts 21:1–14)

[1] Now it came to pass, that when we had departed from them and set sail, running a straight course we came to Cos, the following day to Rhodes, and from there to Patara. [2] And finding a ship sailing over to Phoenicia, we went aboard and set sail. [3] When we had sighted Cyprus, we passed it on the left, sailed to Syria, and landed at Tyre; for there the ship was to unload her cargo. [4] And finding disciples,

we stayed there seven days. They told Paul through the Spirit not to go up to Jerusalem. ⁵ When we had come to the end of those days, we departed and went on our way; and they all accompanied us, with wives and children, till we were out of the city. And we knelt down on the shore and prayed. ⁶ When we had taken our leave of one another, we boarded the ship, and they returned home.

⁷ And when we had finished our voyage from Tyre, we came to Ptolemais, greeted the brethren, and stayed with them one day. ⁸ On the next day we who were Paul's companions departed and came to Caesarea, and entered the house of Philip the evangelist, who was one of the seven, and stayed with him. ⁹ Now this man had four virgin daughters who prophesied. ¹⁰ And as we stayed many days, a certain prophet named Agabus came down from Judea. ¹¹ When he had come to us, he took Paul's belt, bound his own hands and feet, and said, "Thus says the Holy Spirit, 'So shall the Jews at Jerusalem bind the man who owns this belt, and deliver him into the hands of the Gentiles.' "

¹² Now when we heard these things, both we and those from that place pleaded with him not to go up to Jerusalem. ¹³ Then Paul answered, "What do you mean by weeping and breaking my heart? For I am ready not only to be bound, but also to die at Jerusalem for the name of the Lord Jesus."

¹⁴ So when he would not be persuaded, we ceased, saying, "The will of the Lord be done."

---

1. What did the disciples in Tyre say to Paul? Why do you think Paul ignored their counsel and pressed on toward Jerusalem (see verses 3–5)?

_____

_____

_____

_____

_____

_____

2. What prophecy did Agabus give Paul? How did Paul respond when the people urged him to cease his journey (see verses 10–13)?

_____

_____

_____

_____

_____

_____

Paul's Arrest in Jerusalem (Acts 21:26–36)

26 Then Paul took the men, and the next day, having been purified with them, entered the temple to announce the expiration of the days of purification, at which time an offering should be made for each one of them.

27 Now when the seven days were almost ended, the Jews from Asia, seeing him in the temple, stirred up the whole crowd and laid hands on him, 28 crying out, "Men of Israel, help! This is the man who teaches all men everywhere against the people, the law, and this place; and furthermore he also brought Greeks into the temple and has defiled this holy place." 29 (For they had previously seen Trophimus the Ephesian with him in the city, whom they supposed that Paul had brought into the temple.)

30 And all the city was disturbed; and the people ran together, seized Paul, and dragged him out of the temple; and immediately the doors were shut. 31 Now as they were seeking to kill him, news came to the commander of the garrison that all Jerusalem was in an uproar. 32 He immediately took soldiers and centurions, and ran down to them. And when they saw the commander and the soldiers, they stopped beating Paul. 33 Then the commander came near and took him, and commanded him to be bound with two chains; and he asked who he was and what he had done. 34 And some among the multitude cried one thing and some another.

So when he could not ascertain the truth because of the tumult, he commanded him to be taken into the barracks. [35] When he reached the stairs, he had to be carried by the soldiers because of the violence of the mob. [36] For the multitude of the people followed after, crying out, "Away with him!"

---

3. At the advice of James and the other elders in the Jerusalem church, Paul agreed to go through a purification rite in which he reported to one of the priests in the temple. How did the Jews coming from Asia stir up the people when they saw Paul? Why did they believe that Paul had defiled the temple (see verses 27–29)?

_____

_____

_____

_____

4. How was Agabus's prophecy about Paul fulfilled in Jerusalem (see verses 30–36)?

_____

_____

_____

_____

The Plot Against Paul (Acts 23:11–22)

[11] But the following night the Lord stood by him and said, "Be of good cheer, Paul; for as you have testified for Me in Jerusalem, so you must also bear witness at Rome."

¹² And when it was day, some of the Jews banded together and bound themselves under an oath, saying that they would neither eat nor drink till they had killed Paul. ¹³ Now there were more than forty who had formed this conspiracy. ¹⁴ They came to the chief priests and elders, and said, "We have bound ourselves under a great oath that we will eat nothing until we have killed Paul. ¹⁵ Now you, therefore, together with the council, suggest to the commander that he be brought down to you tomorrow, as though you were going to make further inquiries concerning him; but we are ready to kill him before he comes near."

¹⁶ So when Paul's sister's son heard of their ambush, he went and entered the barracks and told Paul. ¹⁷ Then Paul called one of the centurions to him and said, "Take this young man to the commander, for he has something to tell him." ¹⁸ So he took him and brought him to the commander and said, "Paul the prisoner called me to him and asked me to bring this young man to you. He has something to say to you."

¹⁹ Then the commander took him by the hand, went aside, and asked privately, "What is it that you have to tell me?"

²⁰ And he said, "The Jews have agreed to ask that you bring Paul down to the council tomorrow, as though they were going to inquire more fully about him. ²¹ But do not yield to them, for more than forty of them lie in wait for him, men who have bound themselves by an oath that they will neither eat nor drink till they have killed him; and now they are ready, waiting for the promise from you."

²² So the commander let the young man depart, and commanded him, "Tell no one that you have revealed these things to me."

---

5. Paul was arrested but gave a speech to the crowd in defense of his actions . . . thus taking advantage of another opportunity to proclaim the message of Christ. He was then brought before the Sanhedrin, the Jewish ruling council, and also allowed to speak. When that gathering descended into chaos, the commander of the Roman troops took Paul back into the barracks to protect him. What did the Lord say to Paul that night to bolster his spirits? What mission did God say He had in store for Paul (see verse 11)?

---

6. What plan did Paul's enemies devise to get rid of him once and for all (see verses 12–15)?

Sent to Felix (Acts 23:23–35)

23 And he called for two centurions, saying, "Prepare two hundred soldiers, seventy horsemen, and two hundred spearmen to go to Caesarea at the third hour of the night; 24 and provide mounts to set Paul on, and bring him safely to Felix the governor." 25 He wrote a letter in the following manner:

26 Claudius Lysias,
To the most excellent governor Felix:

Greetings.
27 This man was seized by the Jews and was about to be killed by them. Coming with the troops I rescued him,

having learned that he was a Roman. ²⁸ And when I wanted to know the reason they accused him, I brought him before their council. ²⁹ I found out that he was accused concerning questions of their law, but had nothing charged against him deserving of death or chains. ³⁰ And when it was told me that the Jews lay in wait for the man, I sent him immediately to you, and also commanded his accusers to state before you the charges against him.
Farewell.

³¹ Then the soldiers, as they were commanded, took Paul and brought him by night to Antipatris. ³² The next day they left the horsemen to go on with him, and returned to the barracks. ³³ When they came to Caesarea and had delivered the letter to the governor, they also presented Paul to him. ³⁴ And when the governor had read it, he asked what province he was from. And when he understood that he was from Cilicia, ³⁵ he said, "I will hear you when your accusers also have come." And he commanded him to be kept in Herod's Praetorium.

---

7. The commander of the city had Paul escorted to Felix, the Roman governor of the province of Judea. What did the commander recognize about the charges that had been brought against Paul? Why was he sending Paul to him (see verses 26–30)?

_____

_____

_____

_____

_____

_____

8. Why didn't Felix hear Paul's case right away (see verses 34–35)?

_____

_____

_____

_____

_____

_____

REVIEWING THE STORY

Paul was warned by believers in Tyre and Caesarea that if he went to Jerusalem, he would face danger and arrest. Paul responded that he was ready to be bound for the cause of Christ and continued on with his journey to Jerusalem. Once there, he reported to the church leaders about God's work among the Gentiles. Later, Jews from Asia accused Paul of defiling the temple and began to beat him. Roman soldiers broke up the melee and arrested Paul. His enemies plotted to kill him, but their plan was thwarted. The Roman commander arranged to have Paul transported to Caesarea, where he was to be tried by the Roman governor Felix.

9. What did Paul say to the people who warned him that he would face danger in Jerusalem (see Acts 21:13)?

_____

_____

_____

_____

_____

_____

10. How did James and the elders react when they heard Paul's report on God's work among the Gentiles (see Acts 21:20)?

_____

_____

_____

_____

11. How did Paul's nephew thwart the Jewish plot to kill him in Jerusalem (see Acts 23:16–22)?

_____

_____

_____

_____

12. What arrangements did the Roman commander make to transport Paul safely to Caesarea (see Acts 23:23–24)?

_____

_____

_____

_____

APPLYING THE MESSAGE

13. Who is your role model today for standing boldly in the Christian faith—and why?

_____

_____

_____

_____

14. What circumstances or situations make it difficult for you to bear witness for the Lord?

_____

_____

_____

_____

REFLECTING ON THE MEANING

When Paul arrived in Jerusalem, he reported to the church "in detail those things which God had done among the Gentiles through his ministry" (Acts 21:19). His example shows that one of the toughest and most important lessons of ministry we will ever learn is that we do not work for God. Instead, God works _through_ us.

Jesus instructed His followers, "Let your light so shine before men, that they may see your good works and glorify your Father in heaven" (Matthew 5:16). Our role as believers is not to see how much we can get done for God but to give up control, set our priorities aside, and see what God can do through us. The joy in allowing God to work through us is seeing other people glorifying Him as a result. This is why caring for our relationship with the Lord is far more important than worrying about the skills we may offer Him. If we are unwilling to allow God to work through us, we may never see what He is doing around us.

The apostle Paul always gave glory to God for whatever was accomplished. He told the believers in Philippi, "I can do all things through Christ who strengthens me" (Philippians 4:13). To the believers in Colossae he instructed, "Whatever you do in word or deed, do all in the name of the Lord Jesus, giving thanks to God the Father through Him" (Colossians 3:17). To the followers of Christ in Corinth he wrote, "Whatever you do, do all to the glory of God" (1 Corinthians 10:31). Paul was a mighty man of God, but he never let it go to his head. He kept it in his heart and realized the Almighty God was the One who was doing the work.

119

When Paul finished giving his missionary report, the elders of the Jerusalem church rejoiced and also gave glory to God. In doing so, they were following Paul's lead.

JOURNALING YOUR RESPONSE

What might be keeping you from giving full control of your life and priorities over to God so you can be fully transformed by His grace and used for His purposes?

THE TRIALS OF PAUL

Acts 24:1–26:32

GETTING STARTED

What is something that you have been falsely accused of doing?

_____

_____

_____

_____

_____

_____

_____

_____

_____

_____

_____

SETTING THE STAGE

False accusations plagued Paul for most of his public ministry. Throughout the book of Acts, he is hated, hunted, and haunted by charges that were patently untrue. Adding bitter irony to the situation is the fact these false accusations were the work of the Jewish religious leaders of the day—men who were respected and revered for their strict adherence to the law.

Paul had evangelized the lost. He had confronted false religions when he encountered them in his travels. He had founded churches and reached out to the Gentiles. He had discipled and mentored faithful servants for the task of spreading the gospel. Yet these tireless efforts only served to stir up a wake of hatred and opposition from the enemies of the gospel. In the book of Acts, this reaches a climax when Paul decides to return to Jerusalem and Jewish leaders from Ephesus stir up the crowd against him . . . resulting in his arrest.

Paul begins his journey through the Jewish and Roman legal systems by being sent under armed guard to Felix, the corrupt and immoral Roman governor of Judea. Felix was hoping that Paul would bribe him to be set free, but this did not happen. Felix ended up procrastinating for so long that a successor named Festus arrived on the scene. He also left Paul in chains . . . and when he did finally hear the case, Paul appealed to be heard before Caesar. This meant that Paul would be sent to Rome, but before that happened, he was first brought before another ruling authority: King Agrippa, the great-grandson of Herod the Great.

Some might view all these court appearances as a disruption of Paul's missionary work. But Paul saw only opportunity, for these appearances allowed him to present the gospel to all of his judges. Felix and Agrippa were almost moved to become Christians themselves—but in the end, they prized their power and authority too much. Their responsibility was to keep the peace among the Jewish people, even if it meant that an innocent man had to suffer. Unfortunately, that innocent man was the apostle Paul.

EXPLORING THE TEXT

The Accusations Against Paul (Acts 24:1–9)

¹ Now after five days Ananias the high priest came down with the elders and a certain orator named Tertullus. These gave evidence to the governor against Paul.

² And when he was called upon, Tertullus began his accusation, saying: "Seeing that through you we enjoy great peace, and prosperity is being brought to this nation by your foresight, ³ we accept it always and in all places, most noble Felix, with all thankfulness. ⁴ Nevertheless, not to be tedious to you any further, I beg you to hear, by your courtesy, a few words from us. ⁵ For we have found this man a plague, a creator of dissension among all the Jews throughout the world, and a ringleader of the sect of the Nazarenes. ⁶ He even tried to profane the temple, and we seized him, and wanted to judge him according to our law. ⁷ But the commander Lysias came by and with great violence took him out of our hands, ⁸ commanding his accusers to come to you. By examining him yourself you may ascertain all these things of which we accuse him." ⁹ And the Jews also assented, maintaining that these things were so.

---

1. When Paul arrived in Caesarea, Felix refused to hear his case until his accusers had arrived. Five days later, Ananias the high priest and a lawyer named Tertullus came to the city. How did Tertullus describe Paul? What charges did he lay against him (see verses 5–6)?

_____

_____

_____

_____

2. What was the reaction of the Jewish witnesses who heard the false testimony against Paul (see verse 9)?

_____

_____

_____

_____

Paul's Defense Before Felix (Acts 24:10–23)

¹⁰ Then Paul, after the governor had nodded to him to speak, answered: "Inasmuch as I know that you have been for many years a judge of this nation, I do the more cheerfully answer for myself, ¹¹ because you may ascertain that it is no more than twelve days since I went up to Jerusalem to worship. ¹² And they neither found me in the temple disputing with anyone nor inciting the crowd, either in the synagogues or in the city. ¹³ Nor can they prove the things of which they now accuse me. ¹⁴ But this I confess to you, that according to the Way which they call a sect, so I worship the God of my fathers, believing all things which are written in the Law and in the Prophets. ¹⁵ I have hope in God, which they themselves also accept, that there will be a resurrection of the dead, both of the just and the unjust. ¹⁶ This being so, I myself always strive to have a conscience without offense toward God and men.

¹⁷ "Now after many years I came to bring alms and offerings to my nation, ¹⁸ in the midst of which some Jews from Asia found me purified in the temple, neither with a mob nor with tumult. ¹⁹ They ought to have been here before you to object if they had anything against me. ²⁰ Or else let those who are here themselves say if they found any wrongdoing in me while I stood before the council, ²¹ unless it is for this one statement which I cried out, standing among them, 'Concerning the resurrection of the dead I am being judged by you this day.' "

²² But when Felix heard these things, having more accurate knowledge of the Way, he adjourned the proceedings and said, "When Lysias the commander comes down, I will make a decision on your case." ²³ So he commanded the centurion to keep Paul and to let him have liberty, and told him not to forbid any of his friends to provide for or visit him.

3. How did Paul defend his actions and summarize the way he lived out his Christian faith (see verses 12–16)?

_____

_____

_____

_____

_____

_____

4. Felix had spent a decade living among the Jews in Palestine, and he could see the charges brought against Paul were religious in nature. What did he decide to do to keep the peace with the Jews while not taking any direct action against Paul (see verses 22–23)?

_____

_____

_____

_____

_____

_____

Paul Appeals to Caesar (Acts 25:1–12)

¹ Now when Festus had come to the province, after three days he went up from Caesarea to Jerusalem. ² Then the high priest and the chief men of the Jews informed him against Paul; and they petitioned him, ³ asking a favor against him, that he would summon him to Jerusalem—while they lay in ambush along the road to kill him. ⁴ But Festus answered that Paul should be kept at Caesarea, and that he himself was going there shortly. ⁵ "Therefore," he said, "let those who have authority among you go down with me and accuse this man, to see if there is any fault in him."

⁶ And when he had remained among them more than ten days, he went down to Caesarea. And the next day, sitting on the judgment seat, he commanded Paul to be brought. ⁷ When he had come, the Jews who had come down from Jerusalem stood about and laid many serious complaints against Paul, which they could not prove, ⁸ while he answered for himself, "Neither against the law of the Jews, nor against the temple, nor against Caesar have I offended in anything at all."

⁹ But Festus, wanting to do the Jews a favor, answered Paul and said, "Are you willing to go up to Jerusalem and there be judged before me concerning these things?"

¹⁰ So Paul said, "I stand at Caesar's judgment seat, where I ought to be judged. To the Jews I have done no wrong, as you very well know. ¹¹ For if I am an offender, or have committed anything deserving of death, I do not object to dying; but if there is nothing in these things of which these men accuse me, no one can deliver me to them. I appeal to Caesar."

¹² Then Festus, when he had conferred with the council, answered, "You have appealed to Caesar? To Caesar you shall go!"

---

5. Felix, in spite of his efforts, failed to keep the peace in Caesarea and was replaced by Festus. What happened that provoked Festus to reopen the case against Paul? What were the Jews actually hoping to do by making their request (see verses 2–5)?

_____

_____

_____

_____

_____

_____

_____

6. Paul knew that to return to Jerusalem was to invite certain death. So what did he do instead? What did making this appeal mean for him (see verses 10–12)?

_____

_____

_____

_____

_____

_____

Paul Before King Agrippa (Acts 26:19–32)

[19] "Therefore, King Agrippa, I was not disobedient to the heavenly vision, [20] but declared first to those in Damascus and in Jerusalem, and throughout all the region of Judea, and then to the Gentiles, that they should repent, turn to God, and do works befitting repentance. [21] For these reasons the Jews seized me in the temple and tried to kill me. [22] Therefore, having obtained help from God, to this day I stand, witnessing both to small and great, saying no other things than those which the prophets and Moses said would come—[23] that the Christ would suffer, that He would be the first to rise from the dead, and would proclaim light to the Jewish people and to the Gentiles."

[24] Now as he thus made his defense, Festus said with a loud voice, "Paul, you are beside yourself! Much learning is driving you mad!"

[25] But he said, "I am not mad, most noble Festus, but speak the words of truth and reason. [26] For the king, before whom I also speak freely, knows these things; for I am convinced that none of these things escapes his attention, since this thing was not done in a corner. [27] King Agrippa, do you believe the prophets? I know that you do believe."

[28] Then Agrippa said to Paul, "You almost persuade me to become a Christian."

²⁹ And Paul said, "I would to God that not only you, but also all who hear me today, might become both almost and altogether such as I am, except for these chains."

³⁰ When he had said these things, the king stood up, as well as the governor and Bernice and those who sat with them; ³¹ and when they had gone aside, they talked among themselves, saying, "This man is doing nothing deserving of death or chains."

³² Then Agrippa said to Festus, "This man might have been set free if he had not appealed to Caesar."

---

7. As Paul was waiting to be sent to Rome for trial, a royal couple named Agrippa and Bernice arrived for a visit in Caesarea. They asked to hear Paul's defense, which the apostle gave to them . . . again seizing the opportunity to preach the gospel. What was the basis of the defense that Paul gave for himself (see verses 19–23)?

_____

_____

_____

_____

_____

8. How did Agrippa respond to Paul's presentation of the gospel? Why couldn't he set Paul free, even though he realized Paul had done nothing wrong (see verses 28–32)?

_____

_____

_____

_____

_____

_____

REVIEWING THE STORY

The Jewish leaders recruited an orator (lawyer) named Tertullus to prosecute Paul. Tertullus built his case on false testimony of witnesses—and on flattering words for Felix, the governor who would decide Paul's fate. Paul represented himself capably, but Felix kept him imprisoned as a favor to the Jews. When after two years Festus succeeded Felix as governor, he agreed to hear Paul's case. Again, Paul defended himself against the false charges brought against him. When Festus, waiting to do the Jews a favor, asked if Paul would be willing to go to Jerusalem to be judged, the apostle invoked his right as a Roman citizen to have his case heard by Caesar. Later, King Agrippa, who came for a visit to Caesarea, also asked to hear Paul's case.

9. What did Tertullus accuse Paul of doing (see Acts 24:6)?

_____

_____

_____

_____

_____

_____

10. What did Felix do to avoid making a ruling either for or against Paul (see Acts 24:22–23)?

_____

_____

_____

_____

_____

_____

_____

11. What reasons did Paul give for wanting his case to be heard before Caesar (see Acts 25:11)?

_____

_____

_____

_____

12. What was Paul's primary goal in making his speech to King Agrippa (see Acts 26:29)?

_____

_____

_____

_____

APPLYING THE MESSAGE

13. In your own experience, what do you find keeps people from making a decision for Christ, even after they have heard the gospel?

_____

_____

_____

_____

14. How can you overcome those obstacles as you present and live out the gospel?

_____

_____

_____

_____

REFLECTING ON THE MEANING

Antonius Felix, the governor of all Judea, came to power during a time of many uprisings and insurrections in Palestine. Like many of the Roman rulers before him, he attempted to navigate this minefield by appealing to the whims of the populace in an effort to keep the peace at all costs. So it is little wonder to read in Luke's account that he was unwilling to offend the Jews by declaring Paul—who he knew was innocent—to be free of the charges brought against him. His solution to the matter was to simply wait and keep Paul in prison indefinitely.

Felix had been given the rare opportunity to hear the truth about Jesus, but instead of acting on that truth . . . he chose to procrastinate. Like many others, Felix failed to take into account the uncertainty of life. Jesus warned about this attitude in a parable when He said, "I will say to my soul, 'Soul, you have many goods laid up for many years; take your ease; eat, drink, and be merry.' But God said to him, 'Fool! This night your soul will be required of you; then whose will those things be which you have provided?'" (Luke 12:19–20). If you could be sure tomorrow will come, perhaps you could wait for another time. But the uncertainty of tomorrow makes procrastinating a dangerous sport.

Procrastination can keep you from acting on defining moments in your life. If you are a Christian, you likely remember the circumstances that brought you to your decision to trust in Jesus Christ as your Savior. There were certain things that happened in that moment that brought you to understand something you would not have accepted before. In that defining moment, God spoke to you. You heard His voice, you *acted*, and you were saved.

You may get a tomorrow, but you have no guarantee that you will hear God's voice at the same level of intensity or that you will have an opportunity to respond to Him. Tomorrow your life may be filled with thoughts of other things that will obscure God's voice. Tomorrow changes everything. It is today that God has spoken. God's Word gives you a message of urgency that when God speaks to you—when He brings you to a place of conviction—He desires you to respond in that moment. If you do not, like Felix, you risk everything.

JOURNALING YOUR RESPONSE

What are some reasons you procrastinate? What steps can you take to overcome the temptation to put off until tomorrow what can be done today?

LESSON *twelve*

THE VOYAGE TO ROME

Acts 27:1–28:31

GETTING STARTED

What is the worst storm that you have weathered in your life?

_____

_____

_____

_____

_____

_____

_____

_____

_____

_____

_____

_____

SETTING THE STAGE

As we come to the closing chapters in the book of Acts, there is a sense of resolution about everything the apostle Paul was now facing. Previously, he had received a vision that he would one day preach the gospel in Rome.

The Lord had said to him, "Be of good cheer, Paul; for as you have testified for Me in Jerusalem, so you must also bear witness at Rome" (Acts 23:11). Paul had waited in Caesarea for this vision to come to pass, speaking first before the governor Felix, then Festus, and then King Agrippa and Bernice.

Now, as we will discover in this next section of Acts, the time had finally come for Paul to make this journey. Paul was delivered to a centurion named Julius, who would serve as his guard, and was boarded on a ship that would sail across the Mediterranean Sea. God had promised Paul that he would end his ministry with the ultimate experience of preaching the gospel in the imperial city, the capital of the Gentile world, and now that was coming to pass.

Along the way, Paul had let it be known that this vision was also in his heart. In his letter to the believers in Rome, he wrote, "I long to see you, that I might impart to you some spiritual gift . . . as much as is in me, I am ready to preach the gospel to you who are in Rome" (Romans 1:11, 15). It is likely that when Paul first prayed for this opportunity, he had no idea what God was going to do to get him there. Paul wanted to go to Rome as a preacher, but God sent him there as a prisoner.

The story of Paul in the book of Acts serves as a reminder that when we pray, we had better expect to be surprised by the answer. God always accomplishes His will, but He always does it in His own way. It is up to us to just trust in Him and obey.

EXPLORING THE TEXT

The Voyage Begins (Acts 27:1–12)

> [1] And when it was decided that we should sail to Italy, they delivered Paul and some other prisoners to one named Julius, a centurion of the Augustan Regiment. [2] So, entering a ship of Adramyttium, we put to sea, meaning to sail along the coasts of Asia. Aristarchus, a Macedonian of Thessalonica, was with us. [3] And the next day we landed at Sidon. And Julius treated Paul kindly and gave him liberty

to go to his friends and receive care. ⁴ When we had put to sea from there, we sailed under the shelter of Cyprus, because the winds were contrary. ⁵ And when we had sailed over the sea which is off Cilicia and Pamphylia, we came to Myra, a city of Lycia. ⁶ There the centurion found an Alexandrian ship sailing to Italy, and he put us on board.

⁷ When we had sailed slowly many days, and arrived with difficulty off Cnidus, the wind not permitting us to proceed, we sailed under the shelter of Crete off Salmone. ⁸ Passing it with difficulty, we came to a place called Fair Havens, near the city of Lasea.

⁹ Now when much time had been spent, and sailing was now dangerous because the Fast was already over, Paul advised them, ¹⁰ saying, "Men, I perceive that this voyage will end with disaster and much loss, not only of the cargo and ship, but also our lives." ¹¹ Nevertheless the centurion was more persuaded by the helmsman and the owner of the ship than by the things spoken by Paul. ¹² And because the harbor was not suitable to winter in, the majority advised to set sail from there also, if by any means they could reach Phoenix, a harbor of Crete opening toward the southwest and northwest, and winter there.

---

1. How did God show favor to the apostle Paul in regard to Julius, the centurion who was put in charge of guarding him and the other prisoners (see verses 2–4)?

2. It was always difficult for ships to navigate this part of the Mediterranean Sea when the winter months approached. What counsel did Paul give to the centurion? What course of action did the centurion ultimately choose to take (see verses 9–11)?

_____

_____

_____

_____

_____

The Shipwreck (Acts 27:21–41)

21 But after long abstinence from food, then Paul stood in the midst of them and said, "Men, you should have listened to me, and not have sailed from Crete and incurred this disaster and loss. 22 And now I urge you to take heart, for there will be no loss of life among you, but only of the ship. 23 For there stood by me this night an angel of the God to whom I belong and whom I serve, 24 saying, 'Do not be afraid, Paul; you must be brought before Caesar; and indeed God has granted you all those who sail with you.' 25 Therefore take heart, men, for I believe God that it will be just as it was told me. 26 However, we must run aground on a certain island."

27 Now when the fourteenth night had come, as we were driven up and down in the Adriatic Sea, about midnight the sailors sensed that they were drawing near some land. 28 And they took soundings and found it to be twenty fathoms; and when they had gone a little farther, they took soundings again and found it to be fifteen fathoms. 29 Then, fearing lest we should run aground on the rocks, they dropped four anchors from the stern, and prayed for day to come. 30 And as the sailors were seeking to escape from the ship, when they had let down the skiff into the sea, under pretense of putting out anchors from the prow, 31 Paul said to the centurion and the

soldiers, "Unless these men stay in the ship, you cannot be saved." [32] Then the soldiers cut away the ropes of the skiff and let it fall off.

[33] And as day was about to dawn, Paul implored them all to take food, saying, "Today is the fourteenth day you have waited and continued without food, and eaten nothing. [34] Therefore I urge you to take nourishment, for this is for your survival, since not a hair will fall from the head of any of you." [35] And when he had said these things, he took bread and gave thanks to God in the presence of them all; and when he had broken it he began to eat. [36] Then they were all encouraged, and also took food themselves. [37] And in all we were two hundred and seventy-six persons on the ship. [38] So when they had eaten enough, they lightened the ship and threw out the wheat into the sea.

[39] When it was day, they did not recognize the land; but they observed a bay with a beach, onto which they planned to run the ship if possible. [40] And they let go the anchors and left them in the sea, meanwhile loosing the rudder ropes; and they hoisted the mainsail to the wind and made for shore. [41] But striking a place where two seas met, they ran the ship aground; and the prow stuck fast and remained immovable, but the stern was being broken up by the violence of the waves.

---

3. Shortly after leaving the port of Phoenix on the island of Crete, the crew ran into a severe storm that threatened to sink the ship. What admonishment and encouragement did Paul give to the crew at this critical time (see verses 21–26)?

_____

_____

_____

_____

_____

_____

4. What ultimately happened to the passengers and the ship? In what way did this reveal to all on board that the Lord God was in control (see verses 39–41)?

_____

_____

_____

_____

_____

Paul's Ministry on Malta (Acts 28:1–14)

¹ Now when they had escaped, they then found out that the island was called Malta. ² And the natives showed us unusual kindness; for they kindled a fire and made us all welcome, because of the rain that was falling and because of the cold. ³ But when Paul had gathered a bundle of sticks and laid them on the fire, a viper came out because of the heat, and fastened on his hand. ⁴ So when the natives saw the creature hanging from his hand, they said to one another, "No doubt this man is a murderer, whom, though he has escaped the sea, yet justice does not allow to live." ⁵ But he shook off the creature into the fire and suffered no harm. ⁶ However, they were expecting that he would swell up or suddenly fall down dead. But after they had looked for a long time and saw no harm come to him, they changed their minds and said that he was a god.

⁷ In that region there was an estate of the leading citizen of the island, whose name was Publius, who received us and entertained us courteously for three days. ⁸ And it happened that the father of Publius lay sick of a fever and dysentery. Paul went in to him and prayed, and he laid his hands on him and healed him. ⁹ So when this was done, the rest of those on the island who had diseases also came and were healed. ¹⁰ They also honored us in many ways; and when we departed, they provided such things as were necessary.

¹¹ After three months we sailed in an Alexandrian ship whose figurehead was the Twin Brothers, which had wintered at the island. ¹² And landing at Syracuse, we stayed three days. ¹³ From there we circled round and reached Rhegium. And after one day the south wind blew; and the next day we came to Puteoli, ¹⁴ where we found brethren, and were invited to stay with them seven days. And so we went toward Rome.

5. Paul was shipwrecked on the isle of Malta, but this did not stop him from pursuing his mission to preach the gospel of Christ. What event happened that made the natives realize that something was different about him . . . and the God he served (see verses 3–5)?

_____

_____

_____

_____

6. What event opened the way for Paul to reveal God's power and preach the gospel of Christ (see verses 7–10)?

_____

_____

_____

_____

_____

Paul Arrives in Rome (Acts 28:16–23)

¹⁶ Now when we came to Rome, the centurion delivered the prisoners to the captain of the guard; but Paul was permitted to dwell by himself with the soldier who guarded him.

¹⁷ And it came to pass after three days that Paul called the leaders of the Jews together. So when they had come together, he said to them: "Men and brethren, though I have done nothing against our people or the customs of our fathers, yet I was delivered as a prisoner from Jerusalem into the hands of the Romans, ¹⁸ who, when they had examined me, wanted to let me go, because there was no cause for putting me to death. ¹⁹ But when the Jews spoke against it, I was compelled to appeal to Caesar, not that I had anything of which to accuse my nation. ²⁰ For this reason therefore I have called for you, to see you and speak with you, because for the hope of Israel I am bound with this chain."

²¹ Then they said to him, "We neither received letters from Judea concerning you, nor have any of the brethren who came reported or spoken any evil of you. ²² But we desire to hear from you what you think; for concerning this sect, we know that it is spoken against everywhere."

²³ So when they had appointed him a day, many came to him at his lodging, to whom he explained and solemnly testified of the kingdom of God, persuading them concerning Jesus from both the Law of Moses and the Prophets, from morning till evening.

---

7. How was Paul treated when he arrived in Rome? What was one of the first things that Paul did when he was in the city (see verses 16–20)?

8. The Jews in Rome had not heard any rumors regarding Paul and were interested in what he had to say. How did Paul take advantage of this opportunity (see verses 21–23)?

_____

_____

_____

_____

_____

REVIEWING THE STORY

The day arrived when Paul would go to Rome to appeal his case to Caesar. The first ship carried Paul and other prisoners around the coast of Asia Minor before landing in Myra. Once there, the centurion in charge found a ship sailing to Italy, and the group made slow progress to the port of Cnidus on the isle of Crete. Paul advised the centurion not to continue, but he wanted to reach the port of Phoenix to winter the ship. A tempest arose, but Paul assured everyone they would survive. They were shipwrecked off the coast of Malta, where they stayed for three months. Paul ministered there until a ship arrived to take him to Rome. Although he remained a prisoner there, he was allowed to receive visitors, including the Jewish leaders of Rome.

9. Why didn't the centurion listen to Paul's warnings not to sail to the port of Phoenix on the island of Crete (see Acts 27:11–12)?

_____

_____

_____

_____

_____

10. What warning did Paul give to those who wanted to abandon the ship (see Acts 27:31)?

_____

_____

_____

_____

11. What did Malta natives assume about Paul when they saw he had been rescued from a shipwreck only to be bitten by a viper (see Acts 28:4)?

_____

_____

_____

_____

12. How did Paul continue his ministry under house arrest in Rome (see Acts 28:17–19)?

_____

_____

_____

_____

APPLYING THE MESSAGE

13. When are some times that others have warned you about a "storm" headed your way? How did you respond to their counsel?

_____

_____

_____

_____

14. How has God miraculously rescued you in your life?

_____

_____

_____

_____

REFLECTING ON THE MEANING

The account of Paul's shipwreck teaches us that there will be storms in the Christian life. The apostle Peter put it this way: "Beloved, do not think it strange concerning the fiery trial which is to try you, as though some strange thing happened to you; but rejoice to the extent that you partake of Christ's sufferings, that when His glory is revealed, you may also be glad with exceeding joy" (1 Peter 4:12–13). In other words, when we go through a storm, we can't say, "God, why me?" God *allows* storms in our lives to strengthen and deepen our faith.

For this reason, we need to approach our storms the way Paul did in his life. As we have seen, he endured *many* storms in life. As he wrote to the believers in Corinth, "Three times I was beaten with rods; once I was stoned; three times I was shipwrecked; a night and a day I have been in the deep; in journeys often, in perils of waters, in perils of robbers, in perils of my own countrymen, in perils of the Gentiles, in perils in the city, in perils in the wilderness, in perils in the sea, in perils among false brethren; in weariness and toil, in sleeplessness often, in hunger and thirst, in fastings often, in cold and nakedness" (2 Corinthians 11:25–27).

Some preachers and teachers today claim that if we are true believers in Christ, we can expect to experience prosperity and happiness in this life—an earthly existence without storms. But this way of teaching does not come from the Word of God. For as we see at the close of the book of Acts, the apostle Paul—the revered writer of most of the New Testament—is in the midst of one of his greatest storms . . . and yet is also in the midst of God's will for his life.

Sometimes God uses storms to correct us. Sometimes He uses storms to teach us something we couldn't learn in any other way. Sometimes He uses storms to get our attention to make a change, and we are forced to leave the safety of our ship behind. Whatever the case, it is probable that if you're a Christian . . . you're in the midst of a storm.

Journaling Your Response

How has God used storms to accomplish good in your life?

_____

_____

_____

_____

_____

_____

_____

_____

_____

_____

_____

_____

_____

_____

_____

_____

_____

_____

_____

_____

_____

LEADER'S GUIDE

Thank you for choosing to lead your group through this study from Dr. David Jeremiah on *The Acts of the Apostles*. Being a group leader has its own rewards, and it is our prayer that your walk with the Lord will deepen through this experience. During the twelve lessons in this study, you and your group will read selected passages from Acts, explore key themes in the book based on teachings from Dr. Jeremiah, and review questions that will encourage group discussion. There are multiple components in this section that can help you structure your lessons and discussion time, so please be sure to read and consider each one.

BEFORE YOU BEGIN

Before your first meeting, make sure you and your group are well-versed with the content of the lesson. Group members should have their own copy of *The Acts of the Apostles* study guide prior to the first meeting so they can follow along and record their answers, thoughts, and insights. After the first week, you may wish to assign the study guide lesson as homework prior to the group meeting and then use the meeting time to discuss the content in the lesson.

To ensure everyone has a chance to participate in the discussion, the ideal size for a group is around eight to ten people. If there are more than ten people, break up the bigger group into smaller subgroups. Make sure the members are committed to participating each week, as this will help create stability and help you better prepare the structure of the meeting.

At the beginning of each week's study, start with the opening Getting Started question to introduce the topic you will be discussing. The members should answer briefly, as the goal is just for them to have an idea of the subject in their minds as you go over the lesson. This will allow the members to become engaged and ready to interact with the rest of the group.

After reviewing the lesson, try to initiate a free-flowing discussion. Invite group members to bring questions and insights they may have discovered to the next meeting, especially if they were unsure of the meaning of some parts of the lesson. Be prepared to discuss how biblical truth applies to the world we live in today.

Weekly Preparation

As the group leader, here are a few things you can do to prepare for each meeting:

- *Be thoroughly familiar with the material in the lesson.* Make sure you understand the content of each lesson so you know how to structure the group time and are prepared to lead the group discussion.

- *Decide, ahead of time, which questions you want to discuss.* Depending on how much time you have each week, you may not be able to reflect on every question. Select specific questions that you feel will evoke the best discussion.

- *Take prayer requests.* At the end of your discussion, take prayer requests from your group members and then pray for one another.

Structuring the Discussion Time

There are several ways to structure the duration of the study. You can choose to cover each lesson individually, for a total of twelve weeks of group meetings, or you can combine two lessons together per week, for a total of six weeks of group meetings. You can also have the group members read just the selected passages of Scripture that are given in each lesson, or they can cover the entire Book of Acts. The following charts illustrate these options:

TWELVE-WEEK FORMAT

Week	Lessons Covered	Expanded Reading
1	The Day of Pentecost	Acts 1:1–2:47
2	Suffering in Jesus' Name	Acts 3:1–4:37
3	Complete Commitment	Acts 5:1–6:15
4	Persecution and Trials	Acts 7:1–8:40
5	The Hunter Becomes the Hunted	Acts 9:1–43
6	The Gospel Comes to the Gentiles	Acts 10:1–11:30
7	The Power of Prayer	Acts 12:1–14:28
8	The Church in Conflict	Acts 15:1–16:40
9	A Courageous Life	Acts 17:1–20:38
10	Persevering for Christ	Acts 21:1–23:35
11	The Trials of Paul	Acts 24:1–26:32
12	The Voyage to Rome	Acts 27:1–28:31

SIX-WEEK FORMAT

Week	Lessons Covered	Expanded Reading
1	The Day of Pentecost / Suffering in Jesus' Name	Acts 1:1–4:37
2	Complete Commitment / Persecution and Trials	Acts 5:1–8:40
3	The Hunter Becomes the Hunted / The Gospel Comes to the Gentiles	Acts 9:1–11:30
4	The Power of Prayer / The Church in Conflict	Acts 12:1–16:40
5	A Courageous Life / Persevering for Christ	Acts 17:1–23:35
6	The Trials of Paul / The Voyage to Rome	Acts 24:1–28:31

In regard to organizing your time when planning your group Bible study, the following two schedules, for sixty minutes and ninety minutes, can give you a structure for the lesson:

Section	60 Minutes	90 Minutes
Welcome: Members arrive and get settled	5 minutes	10 minutes
Getting Started Question: Prepares the group for interacting with one another	10 minutes	10 minutes
Message: Review the lesson	15 minutes	25 minutes
Discussion: Discuss questions in the lesson	25 minutes	35 minutes
Review and Prayer: Review the key points of the lesson and have a closing time of prayer	5 minutes	10 minutes

As the group leader, it is up to you to keep track of the time and keep things moving according to your schedule. If your group is having a good discussion, don't feel the need to stop and move on to the next question. Remember, the purpose is to pull together ideas and share unique insights on the lesson. Encourage everyone to participate, but don't be concerned if certain group members are more quiet. They may just be internally reflecting on the questions and need time to process their ideas before they can share them.

Group Dynamics

Leading a group study can be a rewarding experience for you and your group members—but that doesn't mean there won't be challenges. Certain members may feel uncomfortable discussing topics that they consider very personal and might be afraid of being called on. Some members might have disagreements on specific issues. To help prevent these scenarios, consider the following ground rules:

- If someone has a question that may seem off topic, suggest that it is discussed at another time, or ask the group if they are okay with addressing that topic.

- If someone asks a question you don't know the answer to, confess that you don't know and move on. If you feel comfortable, invite other group members to give their opinions or share their comments based on personal experience.
- If you feel like a couple of people are talking much more than others, direct questions to people who may not have shared yet. You could even ask the more dominating members to help draw out the quiet ones.
- When there is a disagreement, encourage the group members to process the matter in love. Invite members from opposing sides to evaluate their opinions and consider the ideas of the other members. Lead the group through Scripture that addresses the topic, and look for common ground.

When issues arise, encourage your group to think of Scripture: "Love one another" (John 13:34), "If it is possible, as much as it depends on you, live peaceably with all men" (Romans 12:18), and, "Be swift to hear, slow to speak, slow to wrath" (James 1:19).

ABOUT

Dr. David Jeremiah and Turning Point

Dr. David Jeremiah is the founder of Turning Point, a ministry committed to providing Christians with sound Bible teaching relevant to today's changing times through radio and television broadcasts, audio series, books, and live events. Dr. Jeremiah's teaching on topics such as family, prayer, worship, angels, and biblical prophecy forms the foundation of Turning Point.

David and his wife, Donna, reside in El Cajon, California, where he serves as the senior pastor of Shadow Mountain Community Church. David and Donna have four children and twelve grandchildren.

In 1982, Dr. Jeremiah brought the same solid teaching to San Diego television that he shares weekly with his congregation. Shortly thereafter, Turning Point expanded its ministry to radio. Dr. Jeremiah's inspiring messages can now be heard worldwide on radio, television, and the internet.

Because Dr. Jeremiah desires to know his listening audience, he travels nationwide holding ministry rallies and spiritual enrichment conferences that touch the hearts and lives of many people. According to Dr. Jeremiah, "At some point in time, everyone reaches a turning point; and for every person, that moment is unique, an experience to hold onto forever. There's so much changing in today's world that sometimes it's difficult to choose the right path. Turning Point offers people an understanding of God's Word and seeks to make a difference in their lives."

Dr. Jeremiah has authored numerous books, including *The Coming Economic Armageddon, I Never Thought I'd See the Day!, God Loves You: He Always Has—He Always Will, Agents of the Apocalypse, Agents of Babylon, Revealing the Mysteries of Heaven, People Are Asking . . . Is This the End?, A Life Beyond Amazing, Overcomer,* and *The Book of Signs.*

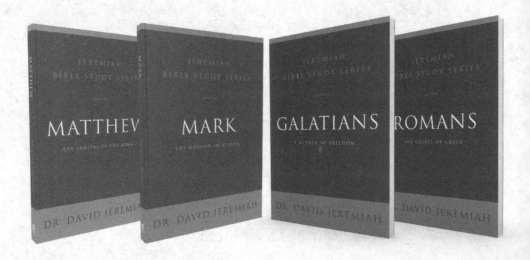